COLLEGE BOUND and MOVING UP!

How Families Launch
First Generation College Students,
And How You Could Help Yours

Mike Santaniello, Ph.D

SophiaOmni

ISBN-13: 978-1463588519

SophiaOmni

Visit our website at:
www.sophiaomni.org

THIS BOOK IS DEDICATED TO MY PARENTS:
MARY (DE RICCO) SANTANIELLO
AND
ANTONIO DOMINIC (TONY) SANTANIELLO,
MY FIRST AND MOST IMPORTANT TEACHERS.

ACKNOWLEDGEMENTS

A special thanks to Linda Beth Alther Santaniello, my best friend and wife of 28 years, for decades of essential input into each and every phase of this project, for our life together, and for being herself. I also owe an eternal debt of gratitude to Professor Herbert J. Gans, for being the most amazing teacher and mentor on the planet. Finally, I must thank Mike Russo for all of his patience, editing help, and assistance, all above and beyond.

TABLE OF CONTENTS

INTRODUCTION

Two young adult Americans, healthy and strong, are about to begin their separate lives. One recently graduated from college, earned a Bachelor's degree and is looking for a job; the other, a high school grad the same age, "works for a living." At this point, the high school grad has what some people mistakenly might call "a good job;" the recent college grad hopes to do better. What are their respective long term prospects of finding fame and fortune, or, at least, some comfort and happiness? The answer will be discussed in the pages that follow.

Do you want your children or grandchildren to have a good life? Of course you do! You love them and care about them! You want them to be comfortable (and more than comfortable) financially. You want them to have good jobs, be treated well, and to enjoy their work. Do you enjoy your work? Are you treated well and with respect? Who gets treated well at their jobs? If you are struggling, do you dream of your children or grandchildren doing better than you are doing? Of course you do!

If you don't have a four year college degree and have children or grandchildren, this book is for you. If you work, your boss or his boss probably has a four year degree. They both make a lot more money than you do, and you probably know much more about your job and how to do it than they do. What's wrong with that picture? They have power over you, and tell you what to do, but they probably can't actually do the work themselves. Do you daydream about being the boss, instead of having to listen to the boss? How do many bosses today get to be bosses? They're all not related to the big boss, are they? Do their college degrees have anything to do with those cushy positions or those fatter paychecks? Absolutely! There! I said it! College degrees are extremely important to your future success! I will prove to you in this book that getting a four year college degree is the ticket to a better life for your children or grandchildren.

This book will teach you all you need to know about pushing your children or grandchildren to go to college, get their four year degrees, and then, have a better life. We will examine the lives of 49 families like yours and mine, who all came from the poorer side of town. The parents all were working people who did not go to college, but their children went to college, and now have those better, cushier lives, **because** they earned their four year degrees. What did those parents teach their children that encouraged them to go to college? What could you teach your children or grandchildren to encourage them to go to college? The fact that you are reading these words means that you are at least a little bit curious, aren't you? Keep reading! What do you have to lose? What do you have to gain?

Since I am a college professor, I think that it is very important that young adult Americans today attend college. If they did not, who would pay my inflated salary, and how could I keep my cushy job? If the college age population of the United States suddenly decided to leave school, I likely would have to go back to "working for a living," which I did with pride for almost twenty years. I spent most of those years of my younger adult life driving a truck, delivering refrigerators and washing machines up numerous flights of stairs in places like The Bronx, New York. The rest of those two decades I spent swinging a hammer or using a screw gun as a laborer and carpenter's helper, pumping gas, or working the counter at a doughnut shop. In fact, I have the scarred hands, sciatica, and torn elbow tendons to prove it. You and I went to the same school: The School of Hard Knocks. I also attended The State University of New York at Stony Brook, and Columbia University. I can deliver almost anything to almost anywhere, and I have a Ph.D. in sociology. I currently am a college professor who loves what he does, earns a great living doing it, and has a very secure financial future. I came up the hard way, growing up in a family where "financial" and "secure" never shared the same sentence.

Given that I ultimately failed to achieve my dream of playing professional football, my decision to attend college is what saved me from a lifetime of financial insecurity. It also saved me from a fate that too many American workers today face. They must struggle to continue to earn a living working at physical jobs that become increasingly challenging as their bodies inevitably age and break down.

I still love to work with my hands. I enjoy dabbling in carpentry, and always will. Working off the "Honey Do List" around the house is much less challenging, however, than my helper and I tossing a three hundred pound refrigerator over our heads to clear a banister in a tenement in ninety degree heat. It also is somewhat comforting to know that my wife and I actually could afford to hire someone to do some of the things that need doing. Many "do it themselfers" don't have that luxury, often because they themselves have "no college."

One key purpose of this book is to analyze whether or not earning a four year college degree really is "worth it." We also will investigate together what a young adult American's prospects are today "in the pursuit of happiness" without a college degree. In addition, we will carefully discuss how and why 49 real Americans from "the poorer side of town" were able to attend college, including the author. Finally, the pages that follow will offer some suggestions to help you encourage your child or grandchild to aspire to attend college, and to earn that degree. As we shall see, we will draw upon quite a bit of research and experience (yours and mine) to raise and answer the key questions implicit in these discussions. I welcome you to the first step of a worthwhile journey.

PART ONE

WHY GO TO COLLEGE?

1

LOSING GROUND

To take an educated guess about the future, we must study the recent past. The U.S. government income data is a good place to start. Since 1980, the poorest 20%, lower middle 20%, and middle 20% of American families all have seen their income shares decrease. This is not a good sign, especially because none of these families were rich to begin with. Why this is occurring is important to understand.

Declines in real wages (actual wage increases compared to cost of living increases) have been common in the U.S. since 1980. What has happened is that wages have not increased as much as the cost of living for many workers. Generally, these declines have affected workers without four year college degrees most often, and with the worst consequences. These declines in real wages themselves are due to several different factors, each of which compounds the problem for working families.

UNEMPLOYMENT

One factor reducing real wages for working people is their increasing rates of unemployment, which lowers real wages, sometimes without workers realizing it. If you were a laborer, what would your life be like?

A look at the working life of a laborer provides a simple and clear example of how real wages can decline for workers. A unionized laborer today may earn $20. or more per hour, especially in the urban Northeast. At $20. per hour, if that laborer works 40 hours per week, and 52 weeks per year, he would earn $41,600. per year gross, placing his family firmly in the middle class. Of course, most laborers in the Northeast do not actually earn $20. per hour, work 40 hours every week, and work 52 weeks per year. If our laborer were out of work 10 weeks last year, his gross income would have been $33,600. The typical laborer in this country is more likely to work fewer hours and fewer weeks in the near future, than he was likely to work in the recent past, for reasons we will discuss. So, next year, he might hope to be out of work only 12 weeks, and expect his income to drop to $32,000. Even if his hourly wage increased, in these times that increase is likely to barely keep up with the increase in the cost of living, if that. So, his real wages will decrease, from last year to next year, simply because he worked fewer hours.

Another problem for American working people is that unemployment affects them more severely than it does higher (salaried) workers. During the severe recession of 2008 – 2011, the overall unemployment rate for (all) American workers was around 10% for two full years. That was the highest unemployment rate in the United States in 70 years, since the Great Depression of the 1930's. What is hidden in those statistics is the fact that unemployment rates for high school grads were extremely much higher than for college grads. During the worst twelve month stretch of the recession, the unemployment rate was 12% for high school grads, but less than 5% for four year college grads! So, workers who already earned less were out of work much more often!

THE PHYSICAL DEMANDS AND PHYSICAL COSTS OF PHYSICAL LABOR

A second factor that tends to lower real wages over time, especially for workers who do manual labor, is the physical breakdown of the human body. I can't physically do at age 59 what I could do at age 29, and few people could. What happens to many laborers as they get older is that they work less often because they are injured more often.

Many baseball fans have noted that the same phenomenon occurs in older pitchers, for the same key reason.

Injuries occur more frequently, in part because workers who are growing weaker as they age try to do "what they used to do" at work. Sheetrock has not gotten lighter over the years, for example, and so, if you are a rocker, you must continue to lift the same weight, even though you are physically not as capable of lifting that weight as you used to be. Secondly, injuries cumulate, as do their effects. If you strained an elbow tendon, for example, that slight undetected tear might increase the likelihood of a more serious tear in the future. Similarly, two strains might add up to a tear, or make a serious tear more likely to occur. The hernia that I experienced in my mid forties, for example, was a "cumulative" injury, according to my surgeon.

An additional physical problem if you do hard physical labor is that recovery time increases with age. As someone who has lifted weights can attest, a strain takes longer to shake off when you are forty than when you are thirty. So, if you strain your lower back muscles doing pick and shovel work, you likely would miss more work from such an injury as you grow older.

As every worker knows, avoiding a catastrophic or debilitating injury is in part a matter of luck, as well as being careful at work. Luck relates to time and "the law of large numbers." The longer you work, and the more that you continue to do what you used to do (even though you are physically less capable of doing it), the greater the chances of your luck running out. Once you hurt your back (and you are likely to, if you do hard physical labor), your ability to work in the future has been reduced. It also becomes increasingly more difficult to fully recover from a debilitating injury as you age.

From personal experience, I can clue you in as to what is likely to happen, if and when you have a serious, debilitating injury at work. The first Murphy's Law of Budgeting and Finance is this: the bills will not stop coming in. Just because you are temporarily (you hope) not working does not mean that the bank (mortgage payment), finance company (car payment), or utility company (lights and heat) will let you off the hook. Chances are you may lose your house if you have one. My parents almost lost their house, when my dad was hurt on the job.

Your disability check, if you get one, will take longer to arrive than you might imagine, and perhaps, much longer. My dad waited fifteen months for his disability settlement check to come. You likely may have to fight your boss, the government, or both, for your inalienable right to a check. How many lawyers do you know who will take such a case *pro bono* (for free)? During your idle days, you might relive the nightmare of getting hurt, which happened in a flash. You then wonder: when will the cavalry ever get here?

Employers are fully aware that the human body tends to break down over time. As employers, their "natural reaction" to this phenomenon becomes an additional factor that reduces the real wages of laborers as they age. Since you, as an aging laborer, are becoming less dependable, and less productive, from a business perspective, you are becoming a financial liability for your employer. Unless your boss will keep you on as an experienced hand, to be the permanent "flag man" or to stand around and show everyone else what to do, you will be replaced. If your boss does not replace you, or find something else productive for you to do, (like be the architect, for example), and he still gives you a check, he soon may be replaced himself. If he is a small business owner, he soon may be out of business.

Since you likely will be replaced, who will replace you? If I were a betting man, I would bet that a younger, stronger, hungrier, and perhaps poorer worker will replace you. In some cases, these workers will be immigrants, but to blame immigrants for your physical inability to do your job is ridiculous. The boss' nephew, your former coworker's son, or some college kid on a football scholarship each would fill the bill, and perhaps be treated better than the poor immigrant.

Whoever your replacement is, he will likely be younger, stronger, and physically more capable of doing your job than you will, at least until time inevitably catches up to him, too. He also is likely to be willing to work for less than you were making, especially in a non union situation. Since the decline in union membership in the United States in recent decades is a well documented reality, this reduction in labor costs (at your expense) is increasingly more likely to occur in the future, if recent trends continue.

Once again, the narrow (or narrow minded) view might blame immigrants for all this, but the reality is not that simplistic. Granted, many immigrant laborers are willing to work for less than you, but many of our own grandfathers did so, too, especially if they were immigrants. Younger workers, with few or no family responsibilities, also are willing to work for less, at least initially. Some of your age peers, especially if they are not living "as large" as you are, or are in more desperate straits, also might work for less than you would.

In a nutshell, the reality of being a worker, and especially, an "unskilled" laborer (the U.S. Department of Labor's term, not mine), is this: they always are trying to replace you. If you really want someone to blame, rather than blaming father time, or young upstarts, or student athletes, or hard working immigrants, or age peers living the simple life, or the boss' nephew, or yourself, blame the machine.

LABOR SAVING DEVICES: RELENTLESS TECHNOLOGICAL CHANGES

"Labor saving devices" have been working to reduce the need for workers since the wheel was invented, and probably before. Labor saving devices actually save the costs of labor (paychecks), and wipe out the jobs that labor depends upon for those paychecks. "The machine" today might be a back hoe, a nail gun, a robot welder, an ATM, or a computer. The machine comes in all shapes and sizes, and with many different functions and purposes. The common purpose is the one that impacts workers in many different fields and sectors of the economy, both in the U.S. and throughout the world: to reduce labor costs. This it does rather relentlessly, despite some well meaning but misguided and hopeless attempts to stop it in its tracks. The very futility of trying to stop "progress" indicates that resistance is a colossal waste of both time and energy.

Examples of technological changes that have altered or eliminated jobs are everywhere. At this point, we will briefly analyze the impact of technology on banking, construction, and auto repairs. Technology has impacted "women's jobs" in banking, for the most part, and mostly "men's jobs" in the two other fields. We will begin this discussion with a peek at banking.

Growing up in the 1950's and 1960's, I always wondered why

banks typically were open only when most working people typically were working (9:00 A.M. - 3:00 P.M., Mondays through Fridays). Many banks, it seemed, wanted to be open when it was most convenient for them. By being open a limited number of hours, banks were able to keep their labor costs down. Yet they faced a bit of a dilemma. If they hoped to improve "customer service," they might have to be open longer than nine to three, which would increase their labor costs. Technology eventually helped provide the answer.

The ATM certainly improves the "convenience" of banking "customers," giving them access to their money twenty four/seven. (Since it is their money, why are depositors called "customers?") With the ATM, the bank can be closed, and not have to pay bank tellers' modest salaries. The ATM not only provided some "teller services" without the tellers, but they began replacing tellers, thus "saving" even more labor (costs). Bank mergers and acquisitions (discussed later) also resulted in the closing of many bank branches, eliminating many more bank teller positions.

As a large number of human bank tellers who used to provide "customer service" were losing their jobs to ATMs, some new, higher status, and higher paid "customer service" positions were created: The "C.S.R." ("Customer Service Representative"). Many of those C.S.R. positions required both extensive training, and some education beyond high school. Unfortunately for some bank employees, there were more teller jobs being eliminated than there were new C.S.R. positions being created. As many bank tellers' jobs disappeared, some tellers hoped to "move up" by becoming C.S.R.s. Both the numbers (more layoffs than new positions), and the requirements of the new C.S.R. position worked against the upward aspirations of most bank tellers, however. Banks often would recruit college students and college graduates to fill many of the new C.S.R. positions.

Any fiftysomething year old mechanic still working as a mechanic can tell you a thing or two about technological changes and the auto repair industry. Fuel injection has replaced carburetors. The piece of fine screen "jerry rigged" between the carburetor and the intake manifold (to "atomize" the gas/air mixture) by a *greaser* in the 1950's has been "redesigned." It is called fuel injection. Electronic ignition systems have replaced distributor points. On board computers and exhaust gas analyzers have replaced old fashioned trouble shooting "by feel." Superchargers and turbochargers have gone from hot rod enthusiasts' dreams to mom's mini van and dad's SUV. In most smaller cars, front wheel drive with "transaxles" has replaced rear wheel ("wagon wheel") drive with its old style transmission and drive shaft.

Automotive testing has changed, too. Annual state motor vehicle inspections were mandated and universalized. They also went up a lot in price, and they became much more complicated (with emissions testing and all). Emissions testing equipment itself was invented and reinvented, and certainly has become far more sophisticated. It also is required, and has become far more costly for shop owners to own and maintain and keep "current." Finally, and most ominously, "regular tune ups" are beginning to be replaced by "the one hundred thousand mile tune up interval." I guarantee you this: the "certified automotive technician" performing that task for you today will be armed with much more than the screwdriver and timing light that backyard mechanics once used for almost everything!

What does all this technology really mean? For one thing (and I never thought that I would ever say this), today's cars are more advanced than the cars of the past. Some of them even put out more horsepower and torque with smaller engines and fewer emissions than the big block beasts that I used to drive to excess did. For another, all that technology *is gonna cost ya big bucks.* Finally, any auto mechanic who has survived all these changes, and still is practicing his chosen craft, must have learned a hell of a lot in a million training classes, since he got out of high school. If he didn't learn about all these new technologies (and how to fix them), then he no longer is capable of practicing his craft, and thereby earning his living. Many older mechanics today, it pains me to say, likely are making more trips to the unemployment office than to the parts house. Don't worry: most parts houses today deliver. In fact, a few of those old mechanics probably are making deliveries for parts houses, or working the counter, for a cut in pay.

In construction, there are many ways that technology has eliminated jobs. Today, machines can dig trenches and holes much faster and far more efficiently than people can, thus reducing the number of pick and shovel labor jobs. When sheetrock replaced plaster walls after World War II, it reduced the number of skilled plasterers needed. "Slot Wall," a newer invention, is sheetrock with a fabric finish installed with "tongue and groove" joints that hide the nails or screws. Slot wall reduces the need for spacklers and painters.

Even carpenters are not immune to the negative effects of the labor saving devices. Carpenter's helpers and laborers today often are used to do some of the "horse work" that the higher paid carpenters could be doing and used to do. Laborers actually are *carpenter* saving "devices," not labor saving devices! Technology also has produced some labor saving devices that both make the carpenter's work easier, and reduce the number of carpenters needed. Bang! Bang! Bang! Bang! Bang! I just shot five three inch nails into a roof rafter in five seconds, attaching it to a top plate. Driven by a compressor, attached by a hose, loaded with a cartridge of nails, a nail gun greatly reduces the need for carpenters. It actually uses carpenters (who are using nail guns) to eliminate the need for more carpenters! Since two carpenters can work faster, and do more in an hour, using nail guns, there is no need for five other carpenters, all swinging hammers. What a great invention!

Another technology that reduces the need for construction workers is the manufactured home. Manufactured homes are typically built in factories, shipped, and assembled on job sites. The main point of these homes, once again, is to reduce labor costs. As one carpenter told me: "They deliver the two halves. We screw them together, and we'll be home by lunch time." As these homes get better and more numerous, the number of carpenters at unemployment offices from coast to coast may grow.

Like carpenters, electricians often are replaced by lower paid workers, and technology makes it easier to do so. Electrician's helpers and laborers now are used to perform much of the heavy work that electricians could do. For example, when wiring a new house, much of the most physically grueling work consists of drilling numerous one inch holes in studs in order to "string lines" through them. A heavy duty right angle drill (the "technology") makes the drilling easier, and thus, quicker, and again saves money by saving time. This increases worker efficiency, but decreases hours worked, and thereby, decreases worker pay. The trick to stringing lines is to drill the holes through the studs at the same height. This facilitates pulling the wires great distances through numerous holes and studs. You also need to cut wires and leave slack, so that the electrician can wire outlets and switches. That's his job, and we wouldn't want to intrude upon it, now, would we?

Plumbers and plumber's helpers could tell similar stories, with the same results. As is the case with the other trades, plumbing often requires difficult physical labor. Labor saving people and devices similarly work to reduce the need for workers making "plumber's pay," and thus, eliminate plumbers. Technological improvements in materials often simplifiy installation, and, in some cases, increase the durability of the work, further reducing labor costs. Half moons and other plumber's jokes aside, reducing labor costs often translates into reduced pay and loss of jobs for workers who lay pipes, fix leaks, and help keep Americans regular.

Masons have experienced population reductions, too. The old ornamental stone work commonly seen on the facades of brownstones and tenements alike was created, on site, by hand, by the Michelangelos of the nineteenth and early twentieth centuries. I recall one artist who signed his work, visible from the BQE (Interstate Route 278) in Williamsburg, Brooklyn: "John Ottati: 1900." These artisans often were viewed (and rightfully so) as among the most skilled by the skilled craftsmen and trades workers of their era. What they once produced, with great care and pride, and never in a jiffy, now is cast in molds and mass produced, so perfectly, and without variation. As was the case with Michelangelo's David, the uniqueness is the point. Something else has been lost here besides skilled jobs.

DO IT YOURSELF

Another labor saving device is the trend towards "do it yourselfing." Today, home centers constantly are advertising "how to" seminars, in which "experts" (perhaps, recently laid off trades people) will teach any *clown* how to hang sheetrock, spackle, lay tile, or anything else that the marketing department can think of. Of course, their prime concern is to get more people into their stores, and more often. From my experiences as a relatively unskilled do it yourselfer, you often end up spending more money and buying more "stuff" if you don't really know what you are doing and still do it yourself. At some point, however, this must reduce the number of hours that real experts actually work hanging sheetrock, spackling, or laying tile.

Technology, as always, puts in its two cents. Pre hung doors, peel and stick floor tiles, slot wall, and put together furniture are among the countless and growing number of labor saving consumer products "for both the professional and the do it yourselfer." These increasingly encourage the clueless to go the do it yourself route and try to add that second floor dormer to a lightly built ranch house, with mixed results. Results will vary, but side effects may include: "the roamin living room" (so named because it now ends up "roamin" all over the house); "the shrinking staircase" (as the house sinks); and "the endless drain" as your project endlessly drains your bank account. Some people spend ridiculous sums of money on "fixer uppers." You might do the same if you do it yourself. The bottom line, once more, is the loss of more building trades jobs. Worry not, for those former carpenters, plumbers, and electricians. They can find jobs working as "experts" on the floors of the giant home center near you, or as installers for those big companies, at reduced pay.

Another aspect of do it yourself involves paying for your materials. Thanks once again to technology, home center customers now can use "self checkout" lanes to scan their own eighty pound bags of cement mix and twenty foot 2 x 10's. Following the lead of "pump your own" gas and "weigh your own" groceries, American retail customers from coast to coast now are doing *for free* what cashiers used to get paid to do.

THE BOTTOM LINE

If you want the bottom line on your long term job opportunities in the building trades, don't listen to me, listen to your federal government. The *Occupational Outlook Handbook*, revised and published every two years, "is a nationally recognized source of career information, designed to provide valuable assistance to individuals making decisions about their future work lives" (page iii). The United States Department of Labor researches and develops this extremely comprehensive, informative, and accurate book. If you have the time, check it out. If you don't have the time, allow me to quote 2004-2005 edition. "Job opportunities for carpenters are expected to be excellent over the 2002-12 period, largely due to the numerous openings arising each year as experienced carpenters leave this large occupation." (page 472) (Question: Why are numerous experienced carpenters leaving each year?) "However, some of the demand for carpenters will be offset by productivity gains resulting from the use of prefabricated components,...As prefabricated components become more standardized, builders will use them more often." (page 472) (Didn't I say that?) "Carpenters can experience periods of unemployment because of the short-term nature of many construction projects and the cyclical nature of the construction industry. Building activity depends on many factors...During economic downturns, the number of job openings for carpenters declines." (page 472) (Translation: Expect to be out of work often.) The outlook for construction laborers is equally rosy: "Job opportunities for construction laborers are expected to be good due to the numerous openings arising each year as laborers leave the occupation." (page 484) (Question: Why are numerous laborers leaving the occupation each year?) "In addition, many potential workers are not attracted to the occupation because they prefer work that is less strenuous and has more comfortable working conditions." (page 484) (Oh, duh, I thought digging holes in the summer was fun!)..."However, employment growth will be adversely affected by automation as some jobs are replaced by new machines and equipment that improve productivity and quality...Employment of construction laborers, like that of many other construction workers, can be variable or intermittent due to the limited duration of construction projects and the cyclical nature of the construction industry...During economic downturns, job openings for construction laborers decrease." (page 484) (No kidding!) In a nutshell, many workers leave the construction field each year due to getting hurt, being worn out, or getting laid off, **and** technology relentlessly eliminates jobs.

I am not suggesting that displaced workers everywhere should affectionately embrace their arch nemesis, the machine. This demon lays them off, and reduces their real wages, far more dependably and systematically than age, injuries, and the boss' nephew combined. I learned a long time ago not to waste energy, although I occasionally still do so, as the love of my life can attest. Trying to fight the on-slaught of technology as it relentlessly marches on is like swimming up Niagara Falls. As I often tell my students: when swimming against the current, sometimes you simply have to change directions.

In the present context, changing directions means the following. First, you must become fully aware that technology eliminates certain jobs, and creates other jobs. Second, you must see that technology is more likely to replace workers who are more easily replaced. Fi-nally, you must understand that workers are at greatest risk of being replaced if their work related tasks are simple for would be replace-ments (human or mechanical) to learn and duplicate.

Once a person understands some of the reasons why he or she should change directions, the next step is choosing the new direction. For that change of direction to be a positive one, the key require-ments are that you move towards the type of job where you perform tasks that are in demand, those tasks are more complex, and the skills you need to perform them are "harder" to learn. For these and other reasons, you then would be harder to replace. Doctors are harder to replace than nursing aides.

MERGERS AND ACQUISITIONS: GONE IN A FLASH

Mergers and acquisitions also have impacted workers in the United States, especially in recent decades. The largest corporations, despite controlling an increasing percentage of the nation's total economic output in recent decades, employ a decreasing percentage of the na-tion's workers. Fortunately, many American workers work for small to mid sized companies, which unfortunately often either go out of business, or are merged or acquired. The reduction of the work forces of the largest corporations is due in part to mergers and acquisitions. Mergers and acquisitions have occurred at a furious pace since around 1980, and continue to do so. Some of the largest mergers and acquisitions have taken place in the defense industry, which still maintains a significant number of industrial jobs within the United States.

Large corporations often are among the largest private employers in their respective geographical areas. In addition to employing thousands of workers directly, countless other jobs in many other companies are due to what some economists call the "multiplier effects" generated by these large employers. Diners, delis, pizzerias, and luncheonettes near where major industrial facilities are located depend heavily on the patronage of workers from these larger local employers. In addition, supply companies from paper goods to uniforms to office machines and computers all grow because of "big company" contracts. Countless other local businesses, from gas stations to grocery stores to card shops, also enjoy a brisk business, due to industrial employees' stops on the way home from work. Even an occasional road repair crew might owe its debt of gratitude (and their jobs) to those thousands of cars, most with one occupant each, wearing out the local roads by ferrying workers from home to work and back.

In the wake of the mergers and takeovers, many thousands of industrial workers as well as some employees of all of those aforementioned dependent local businesses had a new destination: the unemployment office. Engineers, managers, and accountants most certainly were among those given their pink slips, though often with more generous severance packages. The large majority of the workers let go, however, are the masses of workers who actually physically build or assemble the industrial products. Since their hourly wages (and therefore, their severance packages, if any) were lower, their financial situations likely were more precarious than their higher paid salaried coworkers. In addition to losing their jobs, what this larger, poorer group of workers all had in common was what they typically did not have: a four year college degree. Not having a four year college degree made these workers, and millions of others like them, fairly easy to replace. What "being replaced" means for them is that their sometimes precarious financial situations just got a lot more precarious, and fast.

MOVING TO GREENER PASTURES: INDUSTRIAL JOB RE-LOCATION PATTERNS

Some of the workers were replaced by existing employees of the large corporations living in other areas to which those production jobs were relocated. In these cases, the movement of industrial jobs usually conforms to one of the three key patterns of industrial job relocation within the United States that have accelerated since the early 1970's, according the United States Bureau of Labor Statistics. Those patterns of industrial job relocation are: from large, older central cities, to their own suburbs; from metropolitan areas (cities and their suburbs), to non metropolitan areas; and from the older industrial regions of the Northeast and Midwest, to the newer industrializing regions of the Southeast and Southwest. Unfortunately for the former industrial workers of some locales, these three patterns of industrial job relocation are not mutually exclusive. Big, old central cities of the Northeast and Midwest have lost millions of these jobs because all three patterns of change apply to them. New York City alone has lost one million manufacturing jobs between 1950 and 2010. The result has been the emptying out of some older cities, and social and economic devastation in many places. Some of the aforementioned laid off workers, most certainly, were offered the "opportunity" to relocate, and a few did.

In addition to many production jobs being relocated, other jobs were eliminated, as often is the case when two large corporations merge. So, the loss of jobs in one area in these cases was not offset by any real growth of jobs in other areas. (Of course, for those relatively few workers who chose to relocate, their jobs were not lost.) Many American workers over the past two centuries have followed work, moving with jobs or to better job opportunities. As we shall soon see, picking up your family and moving it across the country to follow your job might not be your best option. There certainly is no guarantee that your old job would even remain in this country. In fact, there is the growing likelihood that your job, and many others, might soon be leaving the country, if they haven't already left.

MADE IN CHINA: JOB FLIGHT TO OTHER COUNTRIES

For American workers, especially industrial workers without four year college degrees, a more alarming trend is the increasing number of industrial jobs relocating to other countries. Several major sectors of the American economy have been devastated by this newest pattern of change, including but not limited to textiles (clothing), steel, electronics, automobile production, and computers. This newest wave of globalization generally is favored by much of the government and corporate elites of the United States. Many of the presently industrializing countries possess non democratic governments, lack strong labor movements, and have few, if any government safeguards for workers. These and other factors help reduce labor costs for companies that relocate their production facilities there, compared to what labor costs would be in the United States. In the present climate, how could American workers compete for these jobs with workers from, say, China? The answer is that they cannot, and perhaps, they should not even try. American workers must find something else to do for a living. If they do, they might then become harder to replace.

THE TRICK

The "trick" to becoming harder to replace is no trick. It requires that you obtain or possess some of the more sophisticated skills that fewer people have, and thus, you become harder to replace. A carpenter is harder to replace than a laborer, in part because it takes longer to learn the skills of a carpenter than to learn those of a laborer. In addition, the skills of a carpenter are more sophisticated than those of a laborer. The fact that carpenters are harder to replace does not mean that carpenters cannot be replaced. Instead, what it means is that it will take (or has taken) technology longer to replace carpenters than to replace laborers. As we saw, some of the newer technologies already have begun to replace carpenters, and will continue to do so.

Similarly, and for similar reasons, a nurse is harder to replace than a nursing aide, and a medical doctor is even harder to replace than an orderly. A doctor has earned a Medical degree, which takes considerable time, effort, and expense to achieve. She possesses something that makes her harder to replace, since there are relatively few people with the skills and "licenses" necessary to replace her. That makes her more expensive to replace, and so, she is "worth more," salary wise, being a doctor, than he is "worth," salary wise, being an orderly. In addition, the skills that she possesses are more sophisticated than the skills of her cousin, the orderly. It would take that many more years of "training" to prepare someone else to replace her than it would take to replace him. Finally, his skills are to a significant degree physically based (like the laborer), whereas her skills as an M.D. are primarily mentally based. By using her brain primarily, rather than her brawn, to earn a living, she has insured herself of better long term financial security, as we shall see.

2

UPPING THE ANTE

In the United States today, a substantial number of jobs now require that job applicants have some formal education beyond high school. Many jobs now require at least an Associate's (two year college) degree, and often, a Bachelor's (four year college) degree. What many Americans may not realize, however, is that a growing number of those jobs have raised the minimum education requirement for new applicants, from a high school diploma twenty years ago, to a college degree today. In some fields and situations, new employees with college degrees are working alongside more experienced workers who themselves do not have any formal education beyond high school. In other cases, those younger, less experienced, but college educated workers are replacing their more experienced but less educated co-workers. Prospective employees of a growing number of companies and fields need to know that this is happening, how it is happening, and why it is happening in increasing numbers.

LEVEL OF EDUCATION OVER TIME

According to the U. S. Department of Education, the level of education that the median (middle) adult American over age 25 has attained has been increasing over time for at least fifty years. In recent decades, the rate of increase has increased. For example, the median level of education for an American adult over age 25 in 1945 was 8 years of formal education. By 1985, the median level of education for the same age American adult had risen to more than 12 years of schooling. Any adults in 1985 who had the same education level as their parents had at a similar age, in effect had fallen behind. As the society moved up, any people "standing still" had in effect moved down, relative to other Americans. In most fields, both private and public employers reacted to these changing realities by "upping the ante" for many prospective new employees.

COLLEGE ATTENDANCE RATES, THEN AND NOW

One component of the rising level of formal education among American adults is that both the number and percentage of Americans who attend college has been increasing over time. Today, the majority of American high school graduates attend college. As we might expect, as the number of college students increases, so does the number of college graduates. The percentage of young adults earning Bachelor's degrees has increased substantially, from around 10% in 1970, to more than 25% in 2010. As both the number and percentage of job applicants who have two year or four year college degrees increases, employers "naturally" choose them over their less educated fellow applicants.

YOU NEED SOME COLLEGE TO BE A *WHAT*?

When my dad became a New York City police officer in 1947, some police departments required high school diplomas. Today, a significant and growing number of law enforcement agencies nationwide, including the FBI, U.S. Marshalls, many probation and parole departments, many state police forces, and numerous city, county, and local police forces, now require at least some college, and/or a degree, of all their current and future applicants. Why do so many law enforcement organizations require some college, or even a college degree, of their applicants? In part, the answer simply is because college students are applying for positions in law enforcement. Since so many applicants have two year Associate's degrees (or beyond), why not hire the more educated hopefuls? Since we wish to hire the more educated applicants, why not "make it official," and require all applicants to have Associate's degrees?

There are additional reasons why college educated applicants for law enforcement positions are in greater demand than high school graduates. Despite commonly held myths to the contrary, police work usually involves far more than simply "chasing and arresting the bad guys." Both the training and education that takes place in the various police academies of this nation is substantial. In addition to the academy education, some college education would help to broaden the prospective officer's general knowledge pool. This most certainly would help in the real world of police work, where officers encounter and respond to many different situations on a daily basis.

Police officers responding to a domestic dispute, for example, would be very well advised to know exactly what type of situation they are getting themselves into as they knock on that door. Some working knowledge of psychology certainly would help the officer defuse the situation without further or escalating violence. Having had a sociology course on the family, the officer might be more informed about the statistical likelihood that the abuser or the abused might turn on the responding officer, and what reduces that likelihood. By studying victimology in a criminal justice course, the officer is more likely to understand why the victim might attack the officer, and later, not press charges on her abusive husband. A number of academic disciplines, including the aforementioned, plus social work and nursing, would offer courses (and thereby, insights) into these and other human social situations. For example, the causal relationships among economic stress, alcohol abuse, family history, and domestic violence likely would be understood more fully by a college graduate than by a high school graduate. Which applicant would you hope to see knock on your next door neighbor's door after you "called the cops?"

A police officer who has studied the social and behavioral sciences in college classrooms and field placements would better understand countless other human conditions, social situations, and cultural imperatives. This knowledge couldn't hurt, in the officer's attempt to understand whether or not an individual is behaving suspiciously. Similarly, a working knowledge of "the culture of the street" (Anderson, 1999), from either reading about it, or from experiencing it, would inform the officer how to question someone on the street without showing disrespect. If "dissed," that individual is compelled to respond, and not nicely. Due to my education (a Bachelor's degree, two Master's degrees, and a Ph.D. from Columbia University); and experience (twenty years as a "street kid," fourteen years making home deliveries in the inner city, and twenty five plus years as a college professor and counselor), I am aware of far more situations than I was aware of fresh out of high school. Granted, some of that awareness came from maturity, although some of my students might question how mature I really am! Without a doubt, my education and experiences also broadened my knowledge and understanding of human behavior. I therefore would have been a more effective police officer, if only I could have passed that stupid eye exam.

From my well informed perspective (I teach both criminology, and sociology of the family, and am a cop's son, and grandson), college educated novice police officers are more likely to know what they might run into in domestic or other disputes than high school grad novice officers. To me, that is reason enough to require "some college" of all current and future law enforcement wannabees. The bottom line is, if you wish to wear the blue (or any other color), and become a law enforcement officer, you should go to college.

BACHELOR'S DEGREE REQUIRED FOR INTERVIEW

In the early 1980's, I inadvertently became aware of how some fields were "professionalizing" their work forces. My wife Linda, after completing her Bachelor's degree in education, found her first teaching job, as a temporary one year replacement. After the school year ended, she was not rehired. After searching unsuccessfully for another teaching position, she decided to go into insurance sales. She found numerous insurance sales trainee positions listed in the classifieds of the two major newspapers to which we subscribed. Several major insurance companies, as well as quite a few smaller companies, posted such positions. Many either stated in the ad, or informed her when she called, that "a Bachelor's degree was required for an interview."

Fortunately for us, she possesses that very degree, she interviewed, and she was hired by a major insurance firm.

Linda spend the next several months in an extensive (and fully paid) training program, in which the company informed her about many of their products and services, educated her about sales techniques, laws, and regulations, and prepared her for various licensing and certifying exams. After six months of paid training, she became a successful insurance sales agent. At that time, many of the existing insurance sales agents (some of whom were her coworkers, and many of whom were successful) did not have Bachelor's degrees. Despite the fact that many of the people who already were doing the job successfully did not have degrees, new hires were required to have Bachelor's degrees, in order to even be interviewed. This most certainly is an example of upping the ante to another level entirely.

During the recent era of federal deregulation, the banking and insurance industries both were expanding, and into each other's territories, with a more diversified range of products and services. Apparently, in the "era of the millionaires," these corporations wanted to be certain that their new sales hires actually knew how many zeros there were in a million. One way to insure that your new sales staff would know such pertinent information is to be certain that they have had a math course beyond high school.

More generally, some of the same principles, practices, and rationales that were relevant to the discussion of law enforcement also apply here. Additionally, these corporations wanted to have some assurances that their fully paid trainees would successfully complete their training programs and then go out and make money for the corporations. In this way, the corporation would get some financial return on its sometimes considerable investment of time and money to train these newest recruits for their sales forces. This certainly makes sense, financially speaking. As a growing number of directors of human resources would tell you, one way to insure satisfactory completion of their training program is to hire only candidates who already have completed a certified "training" program.

The Bachelor's degree increasingly is becoming the admissions ticket certifying that its possessor is worthy of entry into the white collar and upwardly mobile sector of the corporate and government worlds. In the not so distant past, people with ability and drive, but without degrees, could move up, and many did so. That pattern of upward mobility soon will be yet another candidate for the history books.

WE WANT OUR MANAGERS TO HAVE BACHELOR'S DE-GREES

Currently, there certainly are many white collar workers in the corporate world who have "good positions," but did not attend college. I personally know dozens of people who have been, or still are, managers, but do not have Bachelor's degrees. Many of these people are "mature adults" with many years of experience. A growing number of these people now are taking college courses, and working towards their degrees. Many managers of similar ages, and without degrees, have been "downsized" or "excessed" out of their management positions. Despite their wealth of experiences, these people now are having great difficulty finding management positions elsewhere at comparable salaries. In a nutshell, three things are happening.

The first is a "natural" expansion of the corporate and government practice discussed earlier in this chapter. As the median level of education continues to rise in the United States, more and more public and private sector employers continue to up the ante. This is happening not only in sales, customer service, and the lower level professions, but also in management and supervisory levels. Thus, new, younger, "management wannabees" must have four year degrees in order to even be considered for a "management trainee" program. Most new hires for management or supervisory positions now have Bachelor's degrees.

The second change is a takeoff from the first. Employers rationalize that, since most of their new managers have degrees, they should then "encourage" their existing managers to earn their degrees. Those upwardly mobiles from the recent past who worked their way up to management without degrees now need degrees to maintain their positions. Some corporations will help in the transformation by paying for some or all of their employees' college tuition. This is a great deal, if you can get it. Other employers are a bit less benevolent. Whether it is mentioned at a department meeting, posted on a bulletin board, written in an email, or whispered at an office party, one thing is certain: "We want our managers to have Bachelor's degrees."

The final step in the "professionalization" of management is easy to figure out. Increasingly, middle age managers who do not possess degrees are being replaced by younger college grads. In this climate, those mature managers with "no college" have three choices: earn their degrees, head south (by requesting a transfer to Antarctica), or go straight to the unemployment office.

At this point in this discussion, you may be thinking: should I get just an Associate's degree (two years), or a certificate of some kind? In a word, the answer is no. Although there are exceptions to the general "No" rule, the rule itself is unyielding. An Associate's degree usually does lead to some increase in income, at least in the short term, over a high school diploma only, but it really is not a great long term solution. If you begin the process of earning your Bachelor's (four year) degree by earning your Associate's degree initially, that is fine. Many Americans complete an Associate's degree first, and then go on to earn a Bachelor's degree or more. One of my former students, whose dad was an electrician, began at the local community college, earned his Associate's degree, transferred to a four year university, earned his Bachelor's, then attended law school, and earned his Law degree. There often are many different roads to the same destination, but getting there is the key. It usually is in your long term best interests to complete the Bachelor's, and the sooner, the better. Even in situations/careers where the Associate's degree leads to a good job (for example, as a police officer), your long term opportunities to be promoted (that is, move up), increase, if you have a Bachelor's degree. This general rule applies in many other fields. In some fields, such as the social services field, people with only Associate's degrees sometimes end up in "management" positions. These positions usually are dead end positions, with titles, but without the significantly higher pay that real "managers" or "directors" come to expect. "Certificates" are similar to Associate's degrees, but at a lower level. If, for example, you earn a "C.A.S.A.C." (Credentialed Alcohol and Substance Abuse Counselor) certificate, you could work as a drug or alcohol counselor, but your opportunities to advance beyond that position would be severely limited. If you had that certificate, plus a Master's Degree in social work, your opportunities would be extensive and much more lucrative. The bottom line is this: if you earn a certificate or an Associate's degree first, that is fine, but **don't stop**. Collect degrees, and you will be much less likely to collect unemployment checks.

THE DUAL LABOR MARKET

The experiences of the typical middle age, high school grad manager who loses his job are the experiences of a person now caught on the wrong side of "the new great divide." Economists call this divide "the dual labor market" or "split labor market." Whatever you call it, it works very simply, and is quite unforgiving.

In the past, an American worker who began as a secretary, stock worker, or sales clerk eventually could "move up" and become a manager, without needing to earn a college degree. Talent, ability, drive, and smarts often were rewarded in this way. Today, what we are witnessing is a "splitting" of the lower levels of corporate and government employment away from the upper levels in the same organization. It is becoming increasingly difficult for an employee to "jump across" the divide without some help.

Help crossing the divide occasionally comes in the form of a well placed friend or relative. In most cases, the only help that the "worthy" employee needs is to earn a four year college degree. If that individual earns that degree, she has become much more promotable, in the current economic circumstances. If he does not earn a degree, then he will be locked in the secondary labor market, where "moving up," getting big pay raises, and gaining job security often are only dreams. It thus seems that earning a four year college degree might be worth the time, trouble, and money it costs to get one. We now turn our attention to asking and answering the question: Is a four year college degree really worth it?

3

EDUCATION AND INCOME

A ny analysis of whether or not it is "worth it" to attend college, and earn a degree, ultimately comes down to money. The "money question" has two components: the financial benefits of earning a four year college degree, and the cost of a college education. As we shall soon see, for virtually every American, the best investment by far that she or he can make is to invest in obtaining a four year college degree. The younger the person is today, statistically speaking, the greater the return on this investment will be. For young children today, the investment in a college education is most critical, for their own financial futures. Their grandparents may or may not have "needed" a college education as desperately, to be ok financially today. Their parents are unlikely to be ok financially today without at least a four year college degree, especially if they currently are young adults. In a nutshell, there is a trend here that we must investigate more fully.

THE INCOME GAP: BACHELOR'S DEGREE VERSUS HIGH SCHOOL DIPLOMA

A perusal of the U.S. government data, available on the U.S. Census Bureau web site, shows us what's happening in gruesome detail. Over time, high school grads, with no degrees completed beyond high school, have seen their average income levels rise since 1975.

That should surprise no one, since cost of living also has risen over that time. Similarly, four year college grads have seen their average incomes increase. At first glance, then, there is no problem, right? Wrong! The problem becomes clearly visible, once we examine several other very interesting realities in these data.

THE SIZE OF THE INCOME GAP

The first noticeable reality is that the gap between the average high school grad, and the average four year college grad, is large. For example, in 1975, the average four year college grad earned $4,489. per year (or $86. per week) more that the average high school grad. As anyone who was trying to support a family in 1975 can attest, $86. per week was "a lot of money" then, especially to a family with less income that their more affluent neighbors. In 1975, the more affluent neighbors were likely to have a four year college degree or two. The less affluent residents of many communities then were more likely to have had high school diplomas only. The average high school grad, in 1975, earned 64% of the income of the average four year college grad, which is not very good, given that they both had to try to support their respective families.

THE INCOME GAP PERSISTS, AND INCREASES OVER TIME

Secondly, the income gap between the average high school grad, and the average four year college grad, exists in each and every year since 1975, and thus, it has persisted over a considerable period of time. Concerning the size of the gap itself, the trend is very good, if you are a four year college grad, and extremely scary, if you are a high school grad only. The gap grew significantly over time, as the four year college grad's average income rose at a much faster rate than the income of the average high school grad did. The average high school grad's income, compared to the average college grad's income, shrunk: from 64% in 1975, to 58% in 1985, to 54% in 2007. In actual dollars, the gap grew from $4,489. in 1975, to $10,420. in 1985, to $25,895. in 2007! Today, the average adult with a high school diploma only earns approximately half as much money each hour, each day, and each week, as the average four year college grad.

THE INCOME GAP, AND THE COST OF LIVING

In addition to analyzing income changes in actual dollars (dollars earned each year), over time, the federal government brings cost of living factors into its analysis of trends. Another measure of income, commonly called "constant dollars," includes an analysis of both cost of living changes, and income changes. What the term constant dollars indicates is how people are doing, over time, in real buying power. Are their incomes rising faster or slower each year than the cost of living is rising? Unfortunately for the non college graduates of the United States, the actual income gap is the least of their problems.

When we analyze the income gap over time, in constant dollars, it is much worse that it initially appeared to be, in actual dollars. The respective gaps in real buying power, (inflation adjusted for 2001), between the average high school grad, and the average four year college grad, were: $14,742., in 1975; $17,121., in 1985; and $22,418, in 1999. Having a four year college degree provides a person with more of a cushion against inflation, than only a high school diploma would provide.

Looking at the data from another angle provides an even bleaker picture of the past and future lives of the non college educated. Between 1975 and 1999, the real buying power of the average high school graduate barely increased, from $25,758. in 1975, to $26,099. in 1999, an increase of only 1%. In fact, the real buying power of the average high school graduate actually fell, between 1975 and 1998. On the other hand, the real buying power of the average four year college graduate increased much more significantly. The improvement was from $40,500., in 1975, to $48,517., in 1999, an increase of 20%.

What this means, in practical terms, is quite obvious. Since 1975, high school graduates have barely kept their heads above water, as rising housing, utility, gasoline, and food prices literally have eaten up any increases in their earnings, except for 1%. In the same time period, four year college grads actually have gotten further ahead, relative to the cost of living. Their gains are real, and substantial, as their real incomes rose 20%, on average, over the same time period. Lest we forget, their incomes, on average, already were substantially higher than their less educated friends and relatives.

HOW TO MAKE A MILLION DOLLARS, AND MUCH MORE

In 2011, the projected difference in lifetime earnings, between a young adult who was a high school graduate only, and a person of the same age with a four year college degree, is one million, two hundred thousand dollars! If that four year college graduate had a Master's degree, instead of "only" a Bachelor's degree, he would earn more than an additional one half million dollars more that his high school grad age peer! If she possessed a "professional degree" (like a Medical degree or Law degree), she would earn four and one half million dollars more than the same age high school grad!

Credit union and bank advertisements, in encouraging people to open savings accounts for their children or grandchildren, occasionally have mentioned the gap we have discussed at length. They say something like: "Give Your Kid a Million Bucks: Pay for Her College Degree." So how much will that degree cost today? It depends on where "your kid" goes to college. Many four year college degrees cost less than fifty thousand dollars in 2011. Even if it costs you one hundred thousand dollars for your child's or grand child's four year college degree today, it is an investment with a projected return of one million, two hundred thousand dollars. A four year college degree is a sound initial investment, with future investments then becoming possible.

The four year degree is like the initial down payment to purchase a house. Without a down payment, you typically cannot buy a house. Once you drop the down payment on a banker's desk, you now have obtained the initial benefits of owning your own home (along with the bank, of course). Those benefits include: if the heat doesn't work, you can get it fixed; and you can hang a picture anywhere you wish. Once you begin to pay off your mortgage, you now have access to wealth acquisition, as the equity in your home effectively becomes money in your pocket. Without a down payment, you cannot begin to pay off a mortgage, and begin to acquire wealth, in the form of home equity. You also could improve or upgrade your house, thereby further increasing its value, especially if houses in general are increasing in value. Again, you cannot make this additional investment, unless you initially put some money down as a down payment.

By investing money and time in a four year college degree, the young adult future college graduate can expect to earn more than one million dollars more, on average, than the average high school grad of the same age today. That obviously is one way that the Bachelor's degree is a sound financial investment. The most important way that a four year college degree is a sound investment, however, is that it serves as a minimum requirement, in order for the holder to go on to earn an additional degree or degrees. Without the Bachelor's degree, you cannot earn: a Master's degree, worth an additional half million dollars, over and above the Bachelor's; or a Professional degree, which pushes the gap between its holder and the high school grad up to four and one half million dollars!

IMPROVED FINANCIAL SECURITY, FOR YOU AND YOUR CHILDREN

Earning a good (or very good) living obviously is important, in a society where even air (for your car's tires) costs money. If you were the typical four year college graduate, you likely would be earning much more money on your first job that your high school grad neighbor would be earning on his first job. Imagine how much money a college grad could put away, if she lived as modesty as high school grads often have to live? Clearly, such "surplus income" could facilitate making many good investments for your family's future. As we proved previously, the best investment one could make is to invest in a four year college degree. If you already had done so for yourself, you then would be in a much better position to help your children attend college than the typical high school grad would be. So, improved financial security, for both your family (savings and investments), and for your children's future (college educations paid for), are additional reasons to earn a four year degree.

THE MARRIAGE FACTOR

Whom do Americans typically marry? According to a ton of social research, Americans are likely to marry someone from a similar social class background. What that means, in practical terms, is that a college grad often marries another college grad, and a high school grad often marries another high school grad. This is very significant, when we think about the previous discussions about the income gap between the average high school grad and the average college grad. The family income gap, between two married college grads, and two married high school grads, will be double the individual gap. In 2007, the average college grad couple would have earned $51,790. more than the average high school grad couple earned. That's a lot of dead presidents!

Concerning marriage and money, there are two other considerations. For one, if both you and your spouse were college grads, your family obviously would be better able to weather the various storms that life tosses our way. For example, a layoff of one breadwinner is not as big a deal when the other breadwinner is a college grad. Since each of you would be earning roughly two salaries (that is, roughly twice as much as your high school grad neighbors) you would be better able to manage on one salary for a while. This depends, of course, on whether or not the college grad couple were living large or living modestly.

A second consideration relates to the dating habits of Americans. College grads often marry college grads. If you are a single high school grad, you would significantly improve your own financial situation by marrying a college grad. Some might call this "marrying money" on a more modest scale than we sometimes see in the papers. Hey, why not fall in love with a college grad? If you already are married, and both you and your spouse are high school grads, do not despair. One of you could attend college, and earn a degree. Then, the other one would be married to a college grad!

SOCIETAL FACTORS: NOTES ON GENDER, RACE, AND SOCIAL CLASS

Unfortunately, several other income gaps exist in the United States today, in addition to the gap between the average high school grad and the average college grad. Those gaps are due to factors that generally are beyond the control of individuals in American society. Gender, race, and social class background each affect an individual's ability to earn a living, independent of her or his educational level. This is due in large part to discrimination, against: women; racial and ethnic minorities; and poor and working class people. If you are a member of one of these groups, you will earn less, on average, than a person with the same education level who is not a member of one of these groups. Numerous studies, including many by the U.S. government, have proven that this is true.

How and why gender, racial and social class discrimination all exist is well beyond the scope of this particular book. What could be done on a societal level, to systematically eliminate these inequities, will not be analyzed here. Helping people cope with these inequities is the point of this particular discussion.

The average woman with a four year degree currently does earn significantly less than the average man with the same degree. The same is true for Blacks, compared to Whites; and for people born to working class parents, compared to children of upper class families. If you or your child is a member of one or more of these disadvantaged groups, there is a way to "overcompensate" for gender, racial, and social class discrimination.

Within each of these groups, the income gap due to educational differences still exists. Therefore, women, minorities, and working class people still should push themselves or their loved ones to attend college. If you were born female, for example, you cannot readily change that, except for the "miracles" of modern medical science. As a woman, you would earn much more, on average, if you had your four year degree, than you will with only a high school diploma. Since you are going to be a woman anyway, unless you opt for surgery (Don't!), you might as well have your degree.

The "overcompensation" method now becomes relevant. Since you will be paid less than a man with the same Bachelor's degree, you might as well get a Master's degree. Before you think that I finally have lost my mind, be aware that many women already are thinking along these lines. Since 1970, an increasing percentage of people attending college are female. The majority of college graduates have been women since the mid 1980's. More significantly, the percentage of students in professional programs who are women has increased rapidly since 1975. If this trend continues, in a short time, the majority of law school and medical school graduates will be women. I would guess that all those women doctors and lawyers will be making more than most male orderlies and court officers. They also might be working to change the system that currently pays female lawyers much less than male lawyers, on average.

4

"JOBS" AND "CAREERS"

Although the typical college grad today earns nearly twice as much money per year as the typical high school grad, the monetary rewards might not be the greatest benefit of a college education.

RESPECT

People in all walks of life want to be treated well, and with dignity and respect. In fact, it is an American belief that this should be so. How are medical doctors treated by their patients? Quite often, they are treated with an incredible amount of deference and respect. In fact, the respect that doctors get from their patients is similar to the "respect" that bosses get from their workers (although, probably for different reasons).

Thinking about work, how are workers often treated by their bosses? Unfortunately, workers often are treated with less than dignity and respect. On a typical construction job site, for example, there is a clearly defined ranking system of status and treatment. The supervisor or "G.C." (general contractor) is treated very well by the workers. In fact, the construction workers sometimes "kiss his butt," at least when he is on the job site. (When he is gone, they might dream about kicking his butt.) The carpenters usually are treated better than (or less worse than) the laborers, and the engineer or architect usually is treated very respectfully by all, especially if the boss is around. There is a broader lesson that we can pull from this example.

Generally speaking, the more education (and thereby, the more income) an American has, the better he is treated "on the job." This clearly is due in part to the power relationships both at work, and in American society as a whole. This also is due to the way most Americans think about different occupations, and the people working in them. Numerous studies have proven that most Americans think "professionals" (like doctors, architects, engineers, and college professors) should have the highest status and prestige, among American workers. Similarly, most Americans look upon laborers and stock workers much less favorably, when status or prestige is considered. So, if an American hopes to be treated with dignity and respect, she or he should attend college, and collect a few degrees.

THE MORE DEGREES YOU HAVE, THE MORE CHOICES YOU HAVE

After earning a college degree or two, a person has far more options. You could choose to work in the construction field, either as an architect or engineer (if you have those degrees), or as a laborer (which I did for two years after I had earned my Master's degree). If you earn your Bachelor's degree, but you love to do carpentry, you could choose to be a carpenter, as long as you have the skills. (I know a man who has a Bachelor's degree, and is a roofer.)

With some carpentry knowledge, and a Bachelor's degree, you also could choose to be a construction supervisor, or a general contractor. If instead you decided to open your own home improvement business, with both construction experience, and a Bachelor's degree in business management, you will have a decent chance to be successful. You should be aware, however, of the small business administration's research on the success rates of small businesses. Most new small businesses fail within three years! Even if you know what you are doing, and are successful, you still must compete (constantly) with the huge corporations.

Having studied metropolitan areas and urban planning, I was better educated as to where to buy land, and where to build our house.

With years of varied construction experience, a few degrees, some family connections, and some common sense, I was able to successfully G.C. the job of building our own house myself. The point is, with a degree or degrees, and some construction skills, the choices are yours. Having the freedom to choose how and where you earn your living is a great thing to have in a society like the United States, where freedom clearly is more important than equality.

TIME IS MONEY, BUT FREE TIME IS A BLESSING

As a college grad, you have additional freedoms that the typical high school grad never will have (unless he hits the lottery). One such freedom is choosing how many hours you wish to work. Of course, a truck driver could choose not to work overtime or a sixth day. He cannot choose to work half as many hours next year as he did last year, however, unless he has another source of income (or he just paid off his mortgage yesterday). Because the college grad earns so much more money per hour, on average, than the high school grad, the college grad can choose to work far fewer hours than the high school grad. This can give you more truly free time. A personal example will serve to clarify.

When I was driving a truck full time, I worked approximately 40 hours per week. Because I was attending college full time for much of my trucking career (job), and because I was living very modesty, I chose not to work "the sixth day." In fact, I typically worked three or four days, ten to twelve hours each, depending on the time of the year, and other circumstances. In my last year as a truck driver, 1983, I earned my highest hourly wage as a truck driver: $6.00 per hour. That was nearly twice the minimum wage in 1983: $3.35 per hour. If I had driven a truck in 2010, and earned a similar wage, relative to the minimum wage, I would have earned approximately $15.00 per hour. This would have been approximately $30,000.00 for the year 2010, if I worked approximately 40 hours per week.

Fortunately for me, I was not driving a truck in 2010. Instead, I had two jobs in my career as a college professor. I was a full time, tenured, Associate Professor of Sociology at one New York area college, and an Adjunct Professor of Sociology at a New York area university. I had one full time teaching position, and one part time teaching position. In 2010, I earned approximately $115,000.00, which was approximately four times what I would likely have earned driving a truck. You must be thinking: "he must have worked a million hours per week, to earn that kind of money." Wrong! In 2010, I actually worked, between the two teaching positions, an average of approximately 30 hours per week for the year! This includes all teaching, office hours, advising students, grading, meetings, and all course and test preparation. Like many professors, I worked "full time" during the fall and spring semesters, and "part time" during the summers. By my calculations, I earned approximately $75.00 per hour as a college professor in 2010.

Thus, by being a college professor, I made **four times** the income I would have made driving a truck in 500 fewer hours per year. What could one do with all that "extra" income? In my case, I put some of it into savings, my retirement investments, and land purchases. How could a person spend all that "extra" free time, that is, time not spent working? In my case, I spent some of my extra time spending some of my extra income! In a nutshell, I work fewer hours per week, earn *a lot* more money, and have more free time (and fewer backaches) being a college professor, than I would being a truck driver. If you earn a college degree or two, and choose your field and circumstances wisely, you will spend far more time doing all the things that you really love to do.

Right now, you probably are thinking: "Yeah, but how many people are off three months per year, like professors, and still get paid an annual salary?" Not that many, except for a few *million* teachers, I admit. There are many professionals who make more per hour and per year than most professors, however. Some lawyers earn $100 per hour or more. One close friend of mine, who drove a truck with me for a while, and now is an M.D., earns one thousand dollars per day (for eight hours) plus traveling expenses as a *locum tenens* ("substitute doctor"). Another doctor friend whose dad was a plumber does "professional medical court testimony" as a second job, in addition to her primary job as the medical director of a nursing home. She has to turn court work down, because there is too much of it. She chooses to work more hours than I do, but she and her husband live in a million dollar house and travel a lot. She earns a ton of money. There are numerous other examples. The point is that most professionals earn very good incomes, and some work fewer hours to do it.

"JOBS" VERSUS "CAREERS"

Many Americans have "jobs;" fewer Americans, unfortunately, have "careers." Remember, I worked at jobs (counter help, gas station attendant, truck driver, construction laborer) for nearly twenty years. For the most recent twenty five plus years, however, I have had a career: college professor. Drawing from forty plus years of personal experience, I can summarize the differences between jobs and careers.

In some ways, I liked driving a truck. (It's a good thing that I did, since I did it full time for fourteen full years.) I always was "a people person," so making home deliveries of major home appliances to approximately thirty thousand different families was fascinating and educational. We found ways (some ok, and some dangerous) to have fun on the job. I also enjoyed working in construction in several ways. I did not enjoy building firewalls sixteen feet tall, with double 5/8 inch sheetrock. I did not have fun pumping gas late at night during the winters in New York. I did not find kneeling on the floor scraping the crud from the stools by the counter while the boss stared at me to be fascinating, although it was educational. I did not love to do coffin carries (over your head) of big refrigerators going up three flights in Chinatown, but I had to do them. A job is something that you have to do, even if you do not often love to do it. What I found is that once you earn a degree or two you are more likely to find something that you actually do love to do. If you can earn a living doing it, then you have found "a career."

I clearly have a career today. I love teaching, which I have done at the college and university levels since 1985. To my shock, but not dismay, I enjoy advising students one to one even more than I love being in the classroom. That I make a much better living doing these things than I ever dreamed of making makes me a very fortunate son from a very humble background. I also make much more money than I ever could have made "working for a living." Granted, there are a few things about my career that I dislike, but I don't have to do them very often. Having a "career" and a Ph.D. from Columbia University, I can afford to refuse to ever work at a "job" again.

As a sociologist and college professor, I have studied and discussed these issues numerous times in 25 years. Anyone who is a college grad and works at a job rather than enjoying a career has only himself to blame. Earning a college degree gives a person the opportunity to earn a very good living doing something that he really enjoys doing! The degree is portable, and you can take it with you anywhere, so you can leave a job to pursue a career. In addition to enjoying your work, you could have more free time to enjoy some of life's leisure pursuits. Finally, you will have more discretionary (extra) income to spend on those leisure pursuits. If you are really smart, though, you also will put some of that surplus income away for a rainy day. You also might *invest* it, as *rich* people do, and have that money make money for you while you are sunning yourself on your new *veranda*.

CONCLUSION

If you understand why, then you can deal with any how. Now that we have thoroughly discussed some reasons why your children or grandchildren must go to college, we can move on to a more detailed discussion of how other working people helped make this dream a reality for their children. Remember: if they did it, **you** can do it, **too**!

PART TWO

HOW I DID IT:
A SAMPLE OF ONE

5

DRIVING A TRUCK
TO COLUMBIA UNIVERSITY

What can you learn about sending your children to college from my life? Quite a bit, and I can prove it to you! Much of what my parents did and didn't do you could do for your children or grandchildren. My life growing up in a working class family was very similar to the lives of 48 other people I came to know who grew up in other working class families. These people all were college students whose life stories I learned about while conducting my research for my Doctoral Dissertation in Sociology at Columbia University. **None** of us had parents who were college graduates while we were growing up, yet we **all** attended college. Each of us went to college primarily because of what our parents did or did not do as we were growing up, we will see.

FINANCIAL CIRCUMSTANCES AND DRIVING RUNNING WRECKS

I was born in Brooklyn, New York. My parents and I lived in my grandmother's basement until my parents were able to buy a house with a V.A. mortgage. We moved to Levittown, New York when I was an infant, and I lived in that working class suburb for the next twenty odd years. I grew up, as I like to say now, "a banana peel away from poverty." I lived in the same home with two parents, a father who always had a steady paycheck, a stay at home mom, and the same roof over my head for most of my childhood and adolescence. Those circumstances, in total, put me "way ahead" of many people in American society.

Of course, growing up, I never saw my family as being among the privileged, and in many respects, we weren't. In fact, we were not very well off at all financially. As we will soon see, your financial status most definitely influences, but clearly does not determine, whether you or your child will attend college. A quick but in depth look back at my life will give us some clues about how and why I eventually attended college. Eventually, I earned a Ph.D. degree from one of the most prestigious universities in the world, Columbia University, without previously having inherited a trust fund.

My dad always worked two jobs. He was a carpenter by trade who became a New York City police officer before I was born. He retired from "The Force" when I was a senior in high school. His second job was doing "odd jobs" related to his trade, like installing new storm doors and windows, roofing, finishing basements, and assorted other carpentry. He never charged much for his services, often bartered with friends or relatives, and sometimes worked for nothing but meals. He always was working, it seemed to me. As a teen, I was his unpaid helper. Carrying a million bundles of roofing shingles, one bundle at a time, up a ladder helped me grow up quickly. It also helped me to appreciate how hard some people and my dad really worked. My mom cared for us, insatiably. She cooked (we ate cheap staples and leftovers often); cleaned (you could eat off her floors); and did laundry, which included hanging clothes up to dry on the ropes in the basement and on the clothes lines in the small back yard. (We did not get our first clothes dryer until I was in high school.) She also was her three children's first and most important teacher, although she herself was a high school dropout. My parents paid the mortgage on their small house, paid the gas and electric bill, paid the phone bill, paid the water bill, and usually had no money left, at the end of each month. They did not pay much for their house (my mom loved to tell us that their first mortgage payment in 1952 was $57.00 per month!), but they did not have much, either. They squeezed by each month. In fact, I remember that my parents rarely had a bank account until I was in high school. There simply was never any money left to put into a bank account. Once per month, as early as I can remember, my Mom and I (eventually accompanied by my younger brother, and later, my younger sister) would walk to the post office, and get money orders for the mortgage, utility, and phone bills. Three things stand out, pertaining to my family's financial conditions: the linoleum story, cars, and vacations.

When I was five, my parents needed to replace the cheap linoleum in their bedroom that came with the house. They did not have the twenty five dollars that the linoleum would cost. To get the money, my parents broke open my giant porcelain piggy bank, which I assume I had since I was born. Any time there actually was any money left, my mom put the pennies (and an occasional nickel) into that bank. By age five, I thought I was rich, until that dark day came. The total haul was about $30.00, and my parents bought me some stupid little toy with what was left, after they bought the new linoleum with my trust fund. I never had very many toys, but I never could remember what that toy was. I will never forget that linoleum, though, bought with my life savings. I was bankrupt, and devastated (or so it seemed to me, then). Money was very hard to come by. **KEY LESSON #1**: Saving money for emergencies and necessities is very important.

My dad always had a car, and he always paid $100.00 or less for it, until I turned 19 years old. He bought "clunkers," typically big, old, and broken down looking, as long as they ran ok. My dad had no automotive mechanical aptitudes whatsoever, so he personally could not fix and/or upgrade, never mind restore, those antique wannabees. So, he often drove each bomb until it died. We went to see my very first major league baseball game in one of those running wrecks, and the day trip was eventful. Most boys growing up in the New York City area in the 1950's dreamed of going to their first baseball game. In the dream, Willie Mays or Mickey Mantle smiled at them, tossed them a ball, or signed an autograph. My reality was a little different. My dad and I drove to the Polo Grounds, in the summer of 1962, to see the New York Mets play the Los Angeles ("they never should have left Brooklyn") Dodgers. I remember three things: the Mets lost, Frank Howard (as I remember) hit a home run, and the trip home. On the way to the game, my dad kept saying: "If we make it over the bridge, we'll be ok." Well, we did make it over the bridge (the Throg's Neck), on the way *to* the game. On the way home, in the middle of the center span, the rusty old tank died. My dad, who always had an explosive temper, didn't even curse (a rarity for him), as if he had been there before. We left the car, walked back to the toll booth on the Bronx side, told the cops about the car, and called our next door neighbor. The ride home was completed, riding in the cab of our next door neighbor's huge, red dump truck.

The Vacations story is the shortest one: none. That was the real story. My parents never went on vacation, except for their honeymoon, which was before my time. As a family, we all never went on vacation together, ever. The first time my parents went on any kind of vacation, once I was around, was during the summer after I graduated from high school. That was exactly twenty years since their last vacation, their honeymoon. My dad, my mom, my brother, and my sister went up to Lake George, New York for a few days about a year after my dad retired from the NYPD. They had fun; I stayed home and worked. Don't feel sorry for me, *pull leaze*! I most certainly did not feel deprived in any way. I was thankful that my parents trusted me enough to let me stay home by myself to work. I made good money during that week, and I was saving up to buy my first new car. By the end of that summer, I did buy my first new car, paying half in cash as the down payment. **KEY LESSON #2**: There are more important things to spend money on than vacations, especially if money is tight.

Other than that I like to ramble and tell stories, what can we get from all this? The fact that my brother, my sister, and I all attended college, and all earned at least a four year degree, has nothing to do with my family's financial standing. Truth is we had no financial standing. My parents were not cheap, just frugal, and their frugality did generate some discretionary dollars, although it took "a while" for those pennies and nickels to amount to anything. What they did with those scarce, hard earned dollars provides a lesson to the "Living Larges" of today. They invested their money in their children's futures, and not on improving the cushiness of their own lifestyles.

LONG TERM FINANCIAL PLANNING

My parents, it turns out, actually were natural born financial planners. My dad's major contribution was working. He often worked literally while most other men slept, and slept a few hours per day. He also spent virtually nothing on himself, ever. He thus generated the "surplus income" which was surplus only in my imagination. My mom's role was a dual one. One of her jobs was to try to squirrel away a few pennies, often squeezing six cents out of each nickel. Her other occupation was to develop a long term growth portfolio. She began the process one fine day in the local grocery store by purchasing our first volume of *The Golden Book Encyclopedia* when I was five years old. For the next few months, once per week, as part of the "big shopping" excursion that was our family's one regular family outing, she dropped Ninety Nine Cents (American) on yet another volume, until we had them all. (I remember that, for some reason, she missed a volume one week, but was able to track down a copy of the missing volume eventually.) This modest purchase, it turns out, was one key component of my own personal educational trust fund. I read the encyclopedia, from A to Z, cover to cover, at the age of five. Why did I read the entire encyclopedia? I read those books for several reasons. My dad encouraged me to read. I am very visual, and those books had many pictures, which drew me towards them. I was very interested in animals, especially dogs and dinosaurs, and my mom taught me that I could learn about anything that I was interested in by reading. Naturally, I read the "D" Volume first, and many times thereafter. I learned a lot, and I came to love learning. Finally, and most importantly, my mom began my journey into The Literate World by reading to me, then with me, until I read by myself. She was The Great Educator without a high school diploma. **KEY LESSON #3**: Books will take a child much further than toys will.

Of course, *The Golden Book Encyclopedia* could not help me to understand Einstein's Theory of Relativity in great detail, so my parents bought more encyclopedias. The next one to enter our humble home was the green hard covered, densely packed, small pages of *The Funk and Wagnalls'*. That they bought when I was ten or eleven. Those volumes were followed, before I began high school, by *The Encyclopedia International* and *The Book of Knowledge.* My parents also bought a large, cheap, combination desk with book cases, which filled every spare square inch of wall space in the big upstairs bedroom which I shared with my younger brother. I filled every cubic inch with books. To illustrate what my parents' spending priorities really were I must describe the series of events that led to my brother and me sharing that room.

When my mom gave birth to her second child, my brother, my dad and my Uncle John finished the larger side of the attic. Since my brother and I would share that room, they also thought it fitting that we would share a bed. So, instead of buying two smaller beds, they saved money by buying one full size bed. This was hardly odd to my dad and my Uncle John, who grew up sharing a bed, along with my Uncle Al. That arrangement, fairly common in the slums of New York in the 1930's, placed the two older boys on either side of the bed, with their heads near the head of the bed, and the little brother, sleeping in the middle, with his head near his two brothers' feet. In describing this arrangement in class, I tell my students that "this resulted in the youngest sibling often getting a case of *Athlete's Face!*" Years later, as my brother's considerable wingspan continued to grow like a mutant super weed, I regretted that day, numerous times. I did, however, learn a thing or two about sharing almost everything with my brother. I also learned that, in the dead of winter, the best response to a brother rolling over towards the radiator with all the covers was to let your foot ice a bit, and then jab him in the side with it.

Other than bringing home the bacon (which we rarely ate), what was my dad's role in my long term financial planning? My dad, though a man of few words (except for curse words, which he yelled in two languages), encouraged me to read by being an avid reader himself. To this day, the most vivid image I have of growing up is the one of my dad with his nose buried in either *The New York Daily News* or *The Readers' Digest*. Most of the time that he was home, if he wasn't sleeping, he was reading. He even read while he was eating his breakfast. He never read during supper, which I am certain was my mom's idea. Instead, he talked, or more accurately, yelled and ranted, about current events in the news. For a man with only a high school diploma, he was extremely knowledgeable about so many things, although I later came to believe that his understanding of the social and economic workings of American society was a bit limited. He keenly understood, however, that the single most important thing he could do for my long term financial security was to encourage me to become an avid reader like himself. I did, especially if I was interested in something.

As my siblings and I got older, my parents began to spend what was for them large sums of money on another aspect of their children's long term financial security: Catholic school tuition. Only when I began to think about writing this section of this book did I fully realize how much money that was for them. Granted, this all was helped along by the V.A., which provided my dad with a 30 year fixed rate mortgage at 4%. By the time I was ready to enter fifth grade, my parents were ready to take the plunge, and send us all, beginning with me, to Catholic schools. I attended Catholic schools from fifth grade through high school, as did my brother, and my sister attended Catholic Schools for a large part of her pre teen years. I still remember that my tuition for high school was $400 for ninth grade, and that it rose to $750 for twelfth grade. Recall that my dad, once married, never spent more than $100 for a car until I was 19 years old! Dad owned and drove each $100 car for a few years until he eventually junked it once it needed "a lot of work" done on it. My parents, then, spent far more for my high school tuition that they ever spent in total on *all* of the cars that they ever owned together during their first twenty years of marriage! Paying tuition for my brother and sister often overlapped with paying my tuition. My dad's one big jump in income occurred in 1969, as I was entering my senior year. He retired from NYPD, and began to work at a new full time job, and continued moonlighting occasionally with carpentry odd jobs. My dad's half pay pension, which to my parents was like him working a third job, basically went to pay for Catholic schools for their three children. Talk about living large! **KEY LESSON #4**: Tuition is affordable if you live modestly.

One additional lesson that my parents taught me about finances was that "everybody works here!" I saw that all the time, since I saw my dad so rarely because he worked so much. Likewise, my mom never seemed to rest; she was always working. I also saw how hard they worked to keep a roof over our heads and plenty of good pasta on the table. When I was fifteen, my dad was about to junk another one of his $100 cars. It was a 1959 Plymouth, with a big block V8 that ran ok, but it needed a complete exhaust system. I begged him to keep the car for me; he said no. I responded by saying: "When I'm seventeen, I want to get a car." He replied: "If you want a car, get a job!" I "got a job" at sixteen, bought myself a used car at seventeen, and bought myself that first new car at eighteen (a 1970 Plymouth with the big block 383 cubic inch V8). I bought a second new car for myself at age twenty two (car loan) and a new car (for cash) for my dad when I was twenty five. My mom and my dad taught me **KEY LESSON #5**: There is no free lunch. They emphasized that "everybody works here," and I should expect to work for everything that I hoped to get. I did.

CORRECTING ARCHITECTS, AND STRESSING EDUCATION

My dad should have gone to college, but he didn't. (Did you ever hear that?) When he was in high school, he was an accomplished runner who had one of the best times in the old quarter mile ("400 meters") in New York City. He also did well in high school, studied drafting, among other applied sciences, and was hoping to become an architect. He had a chance to go to college, because he won a track scholarship to Miami of Ohio University. He talked to his dad, who was a New York City police officer, about it. His dad said: "What do ya wanna go to college for? College is for sissies." My dad never went; he learned carpentry, and later became a city cop instead. Lesson learned, but never fully accepted.

Years later, after my dad retired from The Force and went back to construction, he had at least two incidents of which I am aware (and that I personally witnessed) during which he challenged professionals, and won. In one case, we were working together for a commercial construction company in a very old building on Walker Street in lower Manhattan. The building's rear wall was resting against the rear wall of another old warehouse on the next block (White Street). The company which owned both buildings wanted to open a large doorway/passageway in the back walls, thus joining the two buildings. My dad's boss, who knew the owners, was going to get the job, but he had to give a hard bid. He called in an architect, who estimated the walls to be twelve inches thick, maximum. My dad's boss was going to give his hard bid, but my dad jumped in. He told his boss that those walls were much thicker than the architect estimated, possibly as much as twenty four inches thick, in each building. The architect argued with my dad. My dad said that he knew those buildings, built in the mid 1800's, and that he was right. He also asked the architect what he studied in school, and if he had ever even seen one of these old buildings before. By my dad's tone, he was not being "respectful," that is, he was not deferring to the supposed "expert" with the college education. The architect, whose manhood among other things apparently had been questioned, argued vociferously with my dad. My dad insisted that he was right, and would not back down. He pulled his boss aside, and told him that this was a difficult and much more involved job than he realized, and that he would lose money. His boss reconsidered. My dad suggested that he drill a pilot hole and see how thick the walls really were. His boss agreed. My dad walked out, found a hardware store, and bought a twelve inch long masonry drill bit. He put the bit in his *Milwaukee* drill, and drilled a pilot hole as far as the bit would take him, and a bit more. He pulled the bit out, and saw no light at all. He had to get a longer drill bit, but that was the longest that the hardware store stocked. A few days and one special order eighteen inch masonry drill bit later, he still could not see any light. At that point, the architect was beginning to see the light. My dad's boss gave his hard estimate, assuming the walls to be twenty four inches thick in each building. They were.

In the second case, we were working in a building on 23rd Street also in lower Manhattan. We were installing new petitions and some new doors to change the room layout of the ground floor. The architect drew up plans and sketches with new drop ceilings and the locations of the new walls and doors. After looking at the plans, my dad said: "This is all wrong!" The architect came over to him, and they began discussing the job. After a few minutes, the architect had had it with this upstart carpenter, and asked my dad: "Who's the *architect* here?" My dad responded by saying: "Come here. I want to show you something." He walked the architect over to one of the new pre hung steel commercial doors, complete with door buck (frame) that was leaning against one of the old walls. He told the architect that it was "a six eight door" (the door itself measuring 6 feet, 8 inches tall), but that the top of the heavy duty commercial metal door buck was a bit over 7 feet tall. The architect had drawn up a drop ceiling seven feet tall. Thus, the wall angle that would help hold up the drop ceiling would have to be screwed into the metal door buck (a big no no), and the drop ceiling panels would hide the top of the door buck (another big no no). Oops! Another lesson was about to be learned by a college educated "professional" from a high school educated graduate of the Construction School of Hard Knocks. The humbled, now respectful and deferential architect redesigned the plans.

A short time later, after discussing these two incidents with me once again, my dad concluded: "Well, you know, there are plenty of *intelligent boobs* in the world." Permit me to rephrase, with my college educated vocabulary. There are more than a few people with college educations who have little common sense. Many college graduates, in fact, may not be as intelligent as some of the multitudes of high school grads who work for a living every day. I am certain that many of these workers dream of correcting their bosses and "superiors" more than occasionally. My guess is that they might be right, at least once in a while! More importantly, intelligence or lack of it is **not** what prevents many Americans who do not attend college from doing so. Therefore, never assume that you and your children are incapable of doing college. You might be wrong. Like my dad, your children then might be stuck with correcting bosses who make much more money than they do. **KEY LESSON #6**: Many uneducated people are smart enough to go to college.

LEARNING TO SPEAK "LIKE A REAL PERSON"

Despite the strong influences of my dad, my mom probably was more important in encouraging me to go to college. My mom clearly was my first and most important teacher, as moms in this society often are for their own children. As far back as I can remember, and I remember some things from when I was two years old, my mom always chatted with me, and never talked "baby talk" to me. My mom was trying to teach me how to listen to and understand real words, and how to speak to and have intelligent conversations with adults. My mom was soft spoken and mild mannered about almost everything except baby talk. She absolutely **hated** when any person talked to any baby in baby talk. Once, when someone did talk baby talk to my younger brother when I was four or five, my mother went absolutely ballistic and got all bug eyed, yelling: "**Don't talk baby talk to him! I want him to learn real words!**" I jumped out of my shoes, and I never forgot how angry she was that day. It was anger I had never seen in her before or since.

As my students know well, I have no trouble whatsoever talking. My mom had adult conversations with her first born child from a very early age, I suspect. I wasn't overwhelmed by this, in part because my mom was a high school dropout, and thus, was not a walking *Webster's*. I was challenged, and I responded well to challenges, perhaps because my first challenge was such a positive one. I loved talking to my mom, and she quite obviously loved to talk to me. Fittingly, I was the last person to whom she spoke before she left this world. We always talked, throughout my life, about "a lot" of things. We never talked about sex, but we talked about many other subjects often. Usually, we both enjoyed the conversation, in part because it usually *was* a *conversation*, that is, a give and take between two people who respected one another. My mom most definitely helped me develop both my vocabulary and my listening skills.

In addition to chatting with me, my mom always played the radio, and often sang along with the singers. I enjoyed both the radio and her singing, and occasionally, I even sang along with her and Frank Sinatra or Tony Bennett or Johnny Mathis. I quickly grew to love music, and to appreciate several different types of music. My mom, a bit less tolerant of different music styles than I, called me Michael often, especially when I got into "that noise," known to the rest of the world as "rock." Despite her utter intolerance of *Led Zeppelin* and The *Jimi Hendrix Experience*, she ultimately came to appreciate *The Eagles* and *Chicago,* among other "softer" Rockers. So, we even had open discussions about music, at least occasionally. We also had "discussions" about hair: mine. When it was long, she didn't yell at me to cut it, or catch me while I slept. Instead, she tried to explain to me how bad and unkempt it looked, and how much nicer I looked with short hair. I knew that the time for what I used to call "A Hay Harvesting" was approaching when she started calling me Michael before I got one of her "Hair Filibusters." Overall, if I were to describe my relationship with my mom in general terms, I absolutely would say that it was a positive, cordial, open relationship that lasted until she died. In fact, growing up, my mom was my Best Friend, and my mother. **KEY LESSON #7**: Converse with your children, early and often.

STICKBALL VERSUS HOMEWORK

My mom always wanted me to do well in school from the very beginning of my school years. Despite her cooperative and sometimes submissive nature, she was relentlessly inflexible and extremely assertive with me when it came to schoolwork and homework. The war of the homework between mom and me was very short, and she won that war decisively, although I was the big winner in the long run. I remember my first days of first grade well. Each and every day that I came home with homework my mom and I fought a short skirmish. Although the details and weather reports varied, the gist of every single one of those battles was the same. I would come home books in hand and drop them off somewhere on my way out to play stickball, or football, or running bases, or stoopball, or whatever else I could think of. I would be intercepted by a 5 foot two and a half inch Nike missile preventing my carefree sprint out the front door. "Where are you going?" usually was the question. My response was: "Out to play ..." Before I could finish the sentence, she was in my face with "Not until you do your homework." For about the first week or two, I would respond, with something, anything, pleading my case. It was a completely futile attempt at winning my freedom. By my third week of school, I had given up trying to run, jump, negotiate, or sneak my way out. My mom, I thought, was a very tough prison warden. She sat down with me. "Michael" she said. (My mom always called me Michael, whenever she had something important to say to me. Sometimes, I actually listened. That day, I listened very attentively.) Where was I? Excuse my interruption. She said, very assertively: "Michael. You come home from school, you can have cookies and milk, you do your homework, and then you can go out and play." The law had been laid down. I asked no questions, and I didn't even utter a peep in opposition. At that point I knew that this was a life sentence. From that day forward, I always did my homework (after cookies and milk), did it automatically, and did it without her even having to ask if I had any homework. My mom had established The Rules early and often, and enforced them mercilessly. **KEY LESSON #8**: Parents are in charge, not kids.

A child who does his homework every day, soon after school, is much more likely to do well in school than a child who skips homework altogether, or does it kicking and screaming while falling asleep at 10:00 P.M. As we might expect, I did well in school from the very beginning, and usually had good relationships with my teachers. Teachers often "favored" me, or, at least, tolerated me, because I always did my homework, never missed school, and always came to school prepared to do at least a little work. My mom, a high school dropout, simply would not have it any other way. It was her way, or she told my dad, and I never wanted that to happen. She was an Absolute Tyrant, a Brutal Dictator, a President For Life, with her own private Army (actually, Marine Corps) of One. The one thing that I never challenged her about, from the age of six years and three months, was homework. Period, end of conversation. **KEY LESSON #9**: Schoolwork first; play time last.

TEACHERS, COACHES, TIMES TABLES, DIAGRAMMING SENTENCES, AND THE THIRTY FIVE CENTS THESAURUS

The daily practice of mom's homework mantra certainly helped me build positive relationships with my teachers. Part of this also was luck. I was quite fortunate to have numerous good, great, and/or gifted classroom teachers in my life, from kindergarten through my doctoral dissertation defense. At least several of my teachers genuinely **were** gifted, including Mrs. Fox, Mrs. Raynor, Sister de Montfort, Brother Marion, Professor Chukumeriegie, Professor Pete Seybold, Professor Lewis A. Coser, Professor Gerald D. Suttles, and Professor Herbert J. Gans. I was taught to look up to teachers, especially if they were down to earth, and I did this willingly and enthusiastically. Most of my teachers, not being simpletons, responded in kind to my positive, appreciative overtures. Looking back, I remember many positive experiences, and few negative ones. In fact, I did not have any clearly negative experiences with any teacher until I was attending college.

By then, I had developed a thick skin, and thus, could better withstand a negative onslaught from any Intelligent Boob who happened along. Thanks, dad!

My first noteworthy, and at first glance, negative experience with a teacher was sixth grade with Sister de Montfort. Each and every day, she drilled us on word usage. If she had been a real estate salesperson, her three keys to property values would have been Vocabulary, Vocabulary, and Vocabulary. Sister De (I never would have called her that) always had a staunch ally at her side: her trusty (and crusty) Thesaurus. I didn't even know by the end of fifth grade what a thesaurus was, but by the first week of sixth grade I knew: "a dictionary of words with similar meanings (synonyms) and opposite meanings (antonyms)." As part of her particular brand of mind control, she even forced each of us to buy one. Given that my trust fund (yeah, right) was not yet available to me, I paid what seemed like a fortune for my copy: Thirty Five Cents (American). I hated that book, I hated her class, and I even contemplated hating Sister De. Of course, I knew what my mom might say, if I even thought such thoughts: "Michael, you will go to a very hot place some day." (Definitely much hotter than any desert.) So, contemplating my possible cosmic fate, I passed on actually hating Sister De. Let's just say that I did not fully appreciate her then, and leave it at that.

I did hate sixth grade, with no fear of any reprisals. I hated sixth grade so much that it was my absolute worst school year. Immediately after that horrendous school year mercifully ended, I had my most enthusiastic foray into pyromania: I burned all of my books and notebooks into ashes on my parents' front lawn. To this day I do not fully understand why this tiny act of rebellion triggered my dad to curse at me in two languages, after he found ashes in the grass. Years later, in college, some professor uncorked a flood of bad memories from my subconscious mind by saying in class that: "Sometimes, a student will learn a great deal in a class in which he earns a poor grade." My first reaction to that Intelligent Boob was my typical "Yeah, right." Upon closer examination, I saw that this professor was right, and I recognized that sixth grade was by far my most important year in school. I **never** learned more from a teacher who was not a relative by blood or marriage than I learned from *that* woman, until I entered graduate school. I now understand why she drilled us on vocabulary. After all, I have read Richard Wright's *Words as Weapons*, and I still have that lousy Thirty Five Cent Thesaurus, with its own curly yellow pages. Until I bought a much bigger one, I always used that thesaurus whenever I wrote anything, since that fateful year. I guess it had been drilled into me, like mom's homework mantra.

Speaking of drilling, and with all due respects to the "Let the Child Explore" crowd, drilling was a big part of my education before college. There were many years of physical drilling. I did, after all, play some football, and my parents were strict. I often was drilled, since I am extremely pigheaded, had few fears, and had no regard for how collision-induced trauma might affect my body. No current or former serious athlete worth his weight in *Ben Gay* ever underestimated the importance of drilling for athletic success. I have no doubt that lessons learned from my athletic involvements not only helped me to do well in school, but also helped me expend some anger and energy. Athletic drilling, like the "up downs" we did during many football practices, teaches you how to fall and bounce back up. After playing semipro football, I came to realize that the one tenth of a second that up downs shaved off my "bounce back up time" was the difference between tackling someone with your pinkie, and waving bye bye as he took it to the house. In life, everyone falls. The test is whether or not you bounce back up, and how fast you do so.

The drilling to which I now refer is academic drilling, summed up by two terms of which I am keenly and painfully aware: the times tables, and diagramming sentences. In my educational memories, we always drilled. We learned how to multiply and divide, in part, by studying and memorizing the times tables. To this day, I know that seven thirteens are 91. A few years later (I don't remember exactly when), we began to learn some of the finer points and nuances of sentence structure and grammar by diagramming sentences in our sleep. So, from my experiences, education involves work, drilling, memorization, and some more work. **KEY LESSON #10**: Education often is not fun. A teacher's primary role definitely is not to entertain her class. Since both my mom and my dad drilled me, in different ways,

I was comfortable with the structure and clear chain of command that most of my teachers provided. As a little kid, I was brought up with my dad yelling: "Don't go in the street! You could get hit by a car." When I was a teenager, I saw an unsupervised little kid chasing the ice cream truck run into the street, get hit by a car, fly like a bird, and land on the pavement like a peeled banana hitting a brick wall. He lived, and I learned a lesson that day. **KEY LESSON #11**: Have rules, and explain rules to your children! To this day, "Let the Child Explore" to me means that a little kid is running loose, exploring the middle of Hempstead Turnpike while dodging countless speeding cars in the middle of the rush hour. It *ain't* pretty, believe me. Structure, as we shall see, in conjunction with a strong work ethic, does work well.

THE LAST NAIL

Despite all of these very important people and influences encouraging, pushing, compelling, and preparing me to go to college, one brief conversation, above all others, nailed it for me. For that fork in the road minute in a lifetime, I go back to when I was fifteen. My dad was home that day, and so was I. He either was working midnights, or it was a day during which work was forbidden by an Act of Congress and mom alike. We were hanging out at home, and, out of the blue, my dad said to me: "Mike, I've got to tell you something." I responded: "Yeah, Pops, what is it?" He continued: "You've got to go to college. It's really important. But,... but I can't help you with it. We just don't have the money." I looked at him, and saw the pain etched in his stern face. That was the first time I ever saw him almost cry. He didn't even look like that when his father died. Men just didn't cry in my family. Our culture was Italian, working class, and machismo. In that instant, I realized that my dad was telling himself that he was somehow inadequate as a father and chief provider. His very self image was burnt toast. I thought about what I had just witnessed, and quickly came to two conclusions. The first was that college must be **really** important, so I **have** to go. The second was that I have to get it on my own, like that first car that I craved. Rather than being inadequate, my dad truly was exceptional. **KEY LESSON #12**: College is very important! Lesson learned, big time.

FINISHING SCHOOL AND PAYING THE MORTGAGE

Three years after deciding once and for all that I would go to college, I was set to begin my first semester in the fall of 1970. The day the semester began, I destroyed my leg playing touch football in the street. I caught a pass, ran into a parked car which I dented with my thigh, hit the street hard, but still held on to the ball! (Great catch! Hey! Nobody tagged me! I could have scored if I could have stood up!) Since I could not walk for three months, I had to withdraw before I attended any classes. So, I missed my first semester. I restarted in the spring, figuring that I would start to "make up" the credits I had lost by taking 21 credits the first semester. At that point, I still wanted to graduate "on time." I looked at my class schedule (7 classes on Mondays, Wednesdays, and Fridays); my work schedule (3 full days on the trucks Tuesdays, Thursdays, and Saturdays); and Sundays (doing schoolwork), and I decided that I was nuts! So, I revised my plan.

For the next five full years I worked towards finishing my four year degree. I missed one additional semester, and took 12 credits during most of the other semesters. Except for one semester, I went to school for three long Mondays, Wednesdays, and Fridays of classes every semester, and spent three other long days (Tuesdays, Thursdays, and Saturdays) working ten to twelve hours on the trucks. I left the house around 7 A.M. and got home between 6 P.M. and 8 P.M. every day, for six days each week. Vacations from school were spent working five or six full days per week on the trucks. During the semesters, I really thought about quitting school **every other day** of every week. To this day, I ask my students: What do you think I was saying about school, every Monday, Wednesday, and Friday, when I walked in the door at 6 P.M.? ("School S____.") I did have a great schedule for staying in school, however. At the end of each Tuesday, Thursday, and Saturday, spent climbing the stairs of inner city New York walking backwards, carrying refrigerators and washing machines, I sang a very different tune. I often worked with partners who were older, much more broken down and much less athletic than I was. After seeing my future, without school, in their tired eyes, three days per week, like clockwork, I said: "I gotta get the hell out of here!"

Thank God for my boss Pete! He was thrilled with the idea that I was going to college, and occasionally, when he could spare me, I would take off an occasional Thursday (without pay, of course), to write a paper, read, or study for an exam. Since the job was a shape up job, there always were possible replacement workers, somewhere. The busiest season for home appliance deliveries was the summer, which was great for me. I could work sixty hours per week, which I usually did. Our slow season was the winter, which gave me a chance to get ahead with my schoolwork during the winter/spring semesters. I remember once, when classmates found out that I had completed a term paper during the first month of the semester, they laughed at me. I looked right through them, and said: "Look. I work full time. I have four papers to do each semester. If I don't get one done early, I'm dead!" I also cut classes, typically one full day of classes per semester, to work on a term paper. All of these school related activities I usually did at the public library in Levittown. I would pack a lunch, jump in the car, and spend the day. This way, I could avoid all phone calls (distractions); my neighborhood friends, none of whom went to college, and all of whom wanted to hang out; and my mom, who always wanted to talk.

I loved talking with my mom, as I said previously, but neither my mom nor my dad realized how much time it really took to complete all the work to earn a Bachelor's degree. My mom would chat with me if I was there, and break my chain of thought without realizing it. Some of my college courses were hard, and I really had to concentrate. My dad was another story. One time, when I was writing a paper at home, I had notes, papers and books sprawled all over the kitchen table early that morning. My dad, who was "between jobs" (that is, unemployed) that day, wandered in to get breakfast. He saw the table cluttered with my stuff, mumbled at me in two languages, and took his breakfast outside to the covered back porch. After he ate, he passed by on the way to the den, where he would read a lot and watch a little TV. A few hours later, he came in rummaging around and looking for lunch. He scowled at my papers, mumbled again, grabbed his sandwich, and headed out the back door once more. As he again passed by, on his way back to the den, I said: "Hey, Pops!"

He didn't look too thrilled. Around 5 P.M., I'm still at it, and mom was making sauce for supper. My dad had great nostrils, and drifted towards the kitchen one more time. He saw me, still at it, and finally, he had to say something. He said: "Mike, can I ask you a question?" I replied: "Sure, Pops, what is it?" He responded: "What is it that you are doing that takes *all day*?" I was floored by his question, and for one of the few times in my entire life, I was speechless! After what seemed like an eternity, I simply said: "A term paper," but I realize to this day that, respectfully, he had no clue.

Finally, during the fall semester of 1975 I was primed to finally graduate. My dad, who was back working construction by then, got seriously injured on the job. He cut three fingers on his left hand nearly clean off with a power saw. It really wasn't that bad; he was right handed. It was bad enough that he could not work at all for six months. He had been hurt on the job before, but this was the worst. Other times, when he missed a week or three because of his back or a layoff, my folks still were able to make all their bills. His NYPD pension sure helped; it was like a guaranteed paycheck, which any construction worker will tell you is like bread from heaven. This time, however, there simply was not enough money coming in to pay all the bills. We almost lost everything! My parents emptied their small bank account, and I emptied mine. I worked every hour that I could by cutting school a few times, and I helped by paying the mortgage a few times. We squeezed by, and I graduated. In the end, it took me five and a half years to get my four year degree, but I did get it. Once the semester ended, I worked every day and every hour that I could, and eventually, my family got back on its financial feet. My dad eventually went back to work, I bought them a new color TV and some new furniture, and life went on. I started saving money for graduate school, and to buy my folks a new car. **KEY LESSON #13**: Getting a college degree is mostly an endurance test. How much can you endure, and for how long will you have to endure it?

KEY LESSONS

1. Saving money for emergencies and necessities is very important.
2. There are more important things to spend money on than vacations, especially if money is tight.
3. Books will take a child much further than toys will.
4. Tuition is affordable if you live modestly.
5. There is no free lunch.
6. Many uneducated people are smart enough to go to college.
7. Converse with your children, early and often.
8. Parents are in charge, not kids.
9. Schoolwork first; play time last.
10. Education often is not fun.
11. Have rules, and explain rules to your children!
12. College is very important!
13. Getting a college degree is mostly an endurance test.

PART THREE

HOW OTHERS DID IT

6

BEATING THE ODDS: THE "LIFE STORIES" RESEARCH

This section of this book looks at how and why dozens of real Americans from "humble backgrounds" became successful college students. As the research phase of my doctoral dissertation at Columbia University, I individually interviewed 72 adults. Each person whom I interviewed is referred to as a "Respondent." Many of the respondents were young adults; some were middle aged. Each of these adults grew up in "working class" families. This means that their parents typically worked in manual, clerical, or service jobs for most or all of their working lives. Nearly all of the 72 respondents' parents did not attend college; a few attended briefly. Very few had one parent who eventually earned a college degree. Some (48) of the interview respondents either were attending college, or had already graduated from college, at the time of the interview. These I refer to as the "College Student Respondents" or "Students." Most of the remaining 24 respondents had never attended college, and a few had attended college briefly, and dropped out. These interview respondents I call the "Nonstudent Respondents" or "Nonstudents." Most of the interviews lasted for an hour and a half to two hours each, and, in some cases, we chatted informally afterward. I constructed a list of interview questions (called the "Interview Schedule") which guided the interviews. (See Appendix.) Respondents often were asked "open ended" questions, which means that they could respond any way that they wished to respond. Because of the length, depth, and breath of these interviews, I was able to learn quite a bit about the lives of each of these people and their families. In this book, I refer to this study as the "Life Stories" research, since I learned much about these people's life stories during and after the interviews.

Most Americans who grow up in working class families do not earn four year college degrees; some do. In the Life Stories research, I learned about the life stories of 72 adults who grew up in working class families. Some of these people from working class families attended college, and some did not. By conducting this research, I could analyze how and why some working class children did attend college. Since most people from working class families do not attend college, those few who do so "beat the odds," statistically speaking. By understanding how and why **they** beat the odds, we might suggest how others might follow in their footsteps. As we shall see, the key to whether or not these working class children attended college was what their **parents** did and did not do as parents. The difficult financial circumstances of their families did not prevent them from attending college.

7

PARENTAL INFLUENCES

Parental influences are the subject of this chapter. American children in general and working class children in particular often end up in jobs that are similar to their parents' jobs. They also often attain similar amounts of education as their parents. Most working class children do not attend college. Some do. Working class children who do attend college, and earn degrees, far exceed the educational levels of their parents, and typically end up in jobs "much better" than their parents. My Life Stories research found that working class children who attended college were brought up *differently* by their parents than many other working class children. How did their parents influence them to attend college?

There are family specific factors and processes that influence some working class children to attend college. Some working class parents do value education for their children while others do not. Parents who value education also encourage their children to attend college. Working class children who do attend college generally have parents who valued education and had encouraged them to attend college. We will discuss some of the factors that help working class parents successfully transmit these messages about the importance of education to their children. In this way, we will begin to explore how some working class children become successful college students despite the fact that their parents did not attend college. Financial considerations also influence college aspirations for working class children. Other experiences and situational responses also are at work, as we shall see.

In the Life Stories research, I found several big, qualitative differences in family experiences and values between the college students and the nonstudents. These differences indicate two qualitatively different family systems, one typical of the college students' families, and the other common to nonstudents' families. The existence of two qualitatively different family systems is significant. These differences partially explain why some working class children attend college, while many others do not.

HOW DID PARENTS FEEL ABOUT EDUCATION?

What people say they value is one factor that influences their actions. In the Life Stories research, I found that parental values pertaining to education do affect the actions of both parents and their children. Some working class parents clearly do value education for their children, while others clearly do not. Those parents who do value education generally do encourage their children to aspire to attend college. Similarly, those parents who do not value education generally do not encourage their children to aspire to attend college.

Children certainly are not robots who blindly follow their parents' lead in these or other matters. Children choose to emulate or reject what parents and others say or do. They may forge their own trails, seemingly independent of parental influences. Some children whose parents do value and stress education likely will not value education themselves, and may not aspire to attend college. Other children whose parents did not emphasize education or its importance still may elect to attend college. Clearly, there are other influences in addition to parents' value orientation that affect educational aspirations of children.

Children develop their own values, but not in a social vacuum. Children's values develop through a socialization process that typically involves parents among others. Parents, if present, often are the first significant agents of socialization with whom American children interact. Thus, an investigation of working class children's values logically should begin with an assessment of their parents' value orientation.

The large majority of the college students said that both parents "pushed" or "stressed" or "emphasized" or "valued" education, or thought that education was "very important" or "important." In some cases, the college students' parents had encouraged their children to attend college, even though they felt that success was not guaranteed. The students' parents in general typically did not "force" their children to attend college, according to the respondents. Most of the nonstudents reported that neither parent valued, stressed, or pushed education at all; only one nonstudent said that both parents "valued" education.

That working class parents typically did not attend college is one potential obstacle that college bound working class children must overcome if they are to attend college. These parents do not have the direct and personal experiences typical of college educated professionals. Such experiences certify that a college education usually pays off, both in long term financial benefits, and in other ways. In addition, having not experienced applying for and attending college themselves, the parents could not draw upon their own personal experiences to help them guide or inform their children.

The parents of the college students generally valued and emphasized education as if they themselves were college educated. Their value system in this way resembles that of college educated and/or professional parents. This valuation of education helps their children aspire to attend college despite having parents who did not attend college.

WHAT DID PARENTS DO CONCERNING EDUCATION?

What parents do or do not do to stress education for their children is very important. Actions can reinforce values expressed verbally. If parents' actions and words express similar messages, those messages are more readily received by their children. Among working class parents, what actions might be associated with valuation of education?

Showing a strong interest in how your child is doing in school is one type of action that would positively reinforce valuation of education. Owning books, and reading them, may be others. Putting education near the top of one's list of priorities would be yet another. In these and other ways, the actions of the parents of the college students are consistent with valuing education highly. Similarly, the actions of the parents of the nonstudents are consistent with not valuing education.

KEEPING TABS ON CHILDREN

Valuing education may require that parents "keep tabs" on their children, if the parents hope to translate their values into action by their children. Many college students reported that parents had kept a close eye on their academic performance before college. In these matters, the mothers typically were more involved than the fathers. In fact, the mothers of the college students clearly interacted more frequently and more closely with their college bound children than the fathers did.

The mothers' roles generally were similar for both female and male student respondents in these matters. The same generally was true of the roles of the fathers. The students often saw this parental concern, reflected in behavior, as pivotal.

One way to remain aware of how your child is doing in school is to stay in close contact with the child's teachers. Several college students' parents did regularly contact teachers. The college students generally said that their parents' strong interest in their education was one key reason why they did well in school.

The nonstudents' parents did not contact teachers, and generally accepted whatever results their children achieved in school. The nonstudents' parents' behaviors more closely resemble the more typical working class pattern of acceptance of authority figures' power and opinions, particularly teachers and other authority figures in the school system. Their behavior contrasts with the college students' parents' behavior in these matters.

BOOKS AND ENCYCLOPEDIAS IN THE HOME, AND READING AS A HOBBY

In addition to people, having encyclopedias and other books in the home may encourage working class children to read, help them do well in school, and help them to attend college. Interestingly, many of both the college students and the nonstudents said that they had encyclopedias at home. The one significant difference between the college students and the nonstudents was that nearly all of the college students had books other than encyclopedias at home, but only half of the nonstudents did. The presence of books in the home encourages children to read at home.

I asked the college students to describe and discuss their parents' interests and hobbies, and I discovered reading to be one of them. It was the single most common hobby of both the college students' mothers and the college students' fathers. More than one third of the college students, but only one nonstudent, had at least one parent who read as a hobby.

What parents read may not be as important to children as it may be to adults. A child would have to see that the parent is reading in order to investigate what the parent is reading. Children will not automatically emulate their parents' actions, but in order to emulate any action, that action must be taking place. The college students' parents were much more likely to be reading than the nonstudents' parents. They therefore were much more likely to be "modelers" of reading for their children (Cohen 1987).

Growing up, nearly half of the college students also read as a hobby. Half of the students who read as a hobby had at least one parent who read as a hobby. Only two nonstudents read as a hobby. Having parents who value reading; reading frequently; and reading at a young age all help a child do well in school, when that child grows older (Anderson, et al 1985; Chomsky 1972; Dunn 1981).

HELP WITH HOMEWORK, AND "SELF MOTIVATION"

Homework typically is one important component of the American educational system. Since I was investigating family influences concerning education, it seemed logical to discuss homework during the interviews. Satisfactory completion of homework, as well as time spent on homework, both relate to academic success (Keith 1982; Walberg 1985). Qualitative differences between the college students and the nonstudents concerning homework may relate to the process of becoming a future college attender or nonattender.

A larger percentage of the nonstudents than the college students said that they often received help with homework from one or more members of their immediate (nuclear) families, usually parents. Although the difference was not very large, this finding itself surprised me. Except for informing me who specifically helped them with their homework, both students and nonstudents usually did not elaborate about how they were helped.

Most of the college students reported that doing their homework had been a high priority during childhood, and that they did their homework first, before they went outside to play after school. Generally, this behavior pattern began when they began school, and usually, they continued to prioritize in this way, even as college students. Many students also said that their parents always kept tabs on them, to make sure that they did their homework.

This pattern of prioritizing, placing schoolwork first, before recreation and leisure pursuits, was found only among the college students. None of the nonstudents said anything of the sort, even among those whose parents had helped them with their homework. Doing their homework apparently was not a high priority for the nonstudents.

When a child typically does her or his homework seems to be important from a common sense perspective. A parent fighting with a child at 9:00 or 10:00 P.M. to do homework hardly is conducive to that child doing her or his best work. At that point in the day, both parent and child likely are spent. Parents in this situation might be more likely to simply do the homework for the child, to "get it over with." That hardly encourages the child to learn to do homework diligently and promptly. The significance of doing one's homework soon after coming home from school, as the college student respondents typically did, cannot be overestimated.

All but one of the college students who did not get help with homework said that they were "self motivated," knew that their homework "had to be done," described homework as "my job," or said that their "parents made sure" that they did their homework. None of the non-students who did not receive help with homework made any such comments.

Children who do not get help with homework are not all the same. In fact, there are two qualitatively different ways to not help your children. The first way is to show a strong interest, and instill in your children the "self" desire or motivation to do their own homework. This was common among the parents of the college students. As we have seen, that self desire or motivation may have developed because the parents took a strong interest, and kept tabs on their children. The second way of not helping children with their homework simply is to leave children to their own devices, and not show any interest, or care.

The contrast between help and self motivation becomes increasingly more important as working class children get older, I suspect. As these children progress through grades in school, their parents likely gradually become less capable of helping them with schoolwork, given these parents' own often limited formal education levels. Because the parents no longer are in school themselves, they also were less able to keep up with changes in the curriculum. As the parents become less capable of helping directly, the child's own role likely becomes increasingly more important.

TRANSMISSION OF VALUES FROM PARENTS

How are values transmitted from working class parents who value education to their children? One way that parents in general can transmit values to their children is verbally, by what they say. If verbal value transmission is to be successful, there must be some significant and consistent verbal communication between parents and their children. Working class children who attend college are the exception not the norm. In order for working class parents who value education to transmit those values to their children, they must overcome the transmission of alternative messages and values. These are the messages that the large majority of working class children apparently receive from family and peers: limit your expectations and dreams, value work, get a job, and do not aspire to attend college, among others.

How could parents increase the likelihood that their message will be received? One way is to have open channels of communication between themselves and their children. Research indicates that open communication within families is one key to mutual understanding, both between spouses, and between parents and their children (Melville 1988). In addition to value transmission, open communication also facilitates problem solving, the reduction of anxiety, and works to improve the self image of children (Melville 1988).

Within the college students' families, was open communication typical? Furthermore, was open communication significantly more common within the college students' families than within the families of the nonstudents? Does open communication in these families actually help facilitate the students receiving "pro education" messages from their parents? The Life Stories research suggests answers.

RELATIONSHIPS WITH PARENTS

When asked to describe their relationships with their parents, the large majority of the students specifically said (in their own words) that they had "good communication" or "open communication" with one or both parents, and/or that they "could talk to" one or both parents. Twice as many students gave one or more of those responses than all other additional responses combined. Many students told me that they "could talk to" one or both of their parents "about anything." Many of the students spoke of parents who were approachable, and liked conversing with their children. Generally, students told me that they felt that they could talk to their parents, and they often did so.

More students specifically said that they were closer to their mothers than they were to their fathers. That closeness often facilitated virtually unrestricted communication. According to the students' accounts, their mothers spent more time with them than their fathers did, and it often was quality time. More importantly, it was the mothers who were more likely to "check up on" the students, monitoring their academic progress.

Among the students, the greater frequency of interaction with their mothers compared to their fathers is related to their parents' work schedules. Students' fathers were much more likely to work full time, and typically worked for more years than the students' mothers. In addition, the mothers, even when employed outside the home, still were the primary caregivers of children in these families. Based on the respondents' comments, the mothers also appear to be more expressive and openly communicative than the fathers. This pattern of interaction augments the fact that most of the mothers, like most of the fathers, valued education.

Conversation in general and open communication in particular between parents and their children are among the factors increasing the likelihood of future academic success among the children (Graue, Weinstein, and Walberg 1983; Walberg 1984). Children whose parents converse with them openly and frequently typically develop language, reading, and reasoning skills more quickly than children whose parents are less verbally communicative. The development of these skills relates to future academic success (Graue, Weinstein, and Walberg 1983; Walberg 1984).

Only two of the nonstudents spoke of "good" or "open" communication, in any form, between themselves and their parents. This absence of conversation is one piece of evidence suggesting that a strong "home curriculum" was **lacking** in many of the nonstudents' families. Lack of conversational stimulation in childhood can work to impede educational progress (Graue, Weinstein, and Walberg 1983; Walberg 1984).

In describing what they liked about living at home, many students returned to intrafamily relationships, with approximately half of the students saying that they liked, in their words, "talking to" or "the communication with" or "the relationship with" one or both parents. Some of the remaining students had spoken at length about "good" or "open" communication with their parents earlier in the interview. Few of the nonstudents responded in this manner. One third of the students, but only two of the nonstudents, emphasized "family togetherness" and/or "closeness" and/or "company." Communication appears to be the most common aspect of living at home that the students said that they liked.

Since so many of the students stressed communication, closeness, and/or togetherness, I here generally characterize these college students' nuclear families as "relational families." I define relational families as families in which relationships, togetherness, and communication are important and are emphasized. This "relational" type of working class family, I suspect, is more conducive to producing children who eventually will attend college than other types of working class families are.

OTHER ASPECTS OF HOME LIFE

Another aspect of living at home students liked was "security," and/or "stability." From their additional comments and discussions, it became clear that the students usually were referring to emotional security or stability, and not to material or economic stability. Relationships appear to be more important than material things or conditions to the students. Among the nonstudents, such responses were much less common.

Many students said that they "could count on" their families or on members of their families. One aspect of this was that people in their families supported them emotionally. Several students said that their parents were "very supportive" (emotionally). None of the nonstudents spoke of emotional support.

A third aspect of "counting on" their families pertained to financial security and stability. Many students felt that, no matter how "rough things were," the family "would get by." The students' parents in most cases were the source of this aspect of security and stability to the student respondents. Their perception of security and stability often existed despite economic difficulties. Stability was not discussed by any nonstudents, but several discussed financial or physical security.

A significant percentage (33%) of the nonstudents, but none of the students, said that they derived satisfaction from a different aspect of living at home. These respondents referred much more to material things or conditions than to interpersonal relationships. More specifically, what was important to these nonstudents was that they did not have many responsibilities at home, and that other people, in their words, did "everything" for them.

Nonstudents were much more likely than students to make comments that indicated that they lacked emotional support at home. This lack of emotional support sometimes adversely affected the nonstudents' conceptions of themselves.

PARENTS' WORK EXPERIENCES: MORE HARD WORK AND LESS MOBILITY

In addition to their roles pertaining to education, parents are important agents of socialization in another respect. Intentionally or unintentionally, parents can educate and socialize their children by their actions. This process pertains to work, among other aspects of social life. Life experiences and situational responses also are likely to be influential.

What children envision as possible or not possible is strongly influenced by what they believe does or does not exist in the real world. What they believe exists is based in large measure on what they see. If children are more keenly aware of their parents' work experiences, they then have a somewhat clearer image of how their parents earn a living. Based primarily on those images that are within their fields of vision, they then formulate a more general conception of the work world, including what earning a living is, and how the process typically operates. By investigating the work experiences of the parents, I could begin to understand whether or not the parents' work experiences influenced the respondents' educational or life aspirations.

It is possible that differences in work experiences within the working class help create differences in values within the working class. Differences in parents' value orientation within the working class may help explain differences in educational aspirations and attainment among their children.

As working class adults, the parents of both the students and nonstudents often had similar work experiences, in some respects. In other respects, the work experiences of the students' fathers were qualitatively different from the work experiences of the nonstudents' fathers. In addition, the students' perceptions of their parents' work experiences were different, and more detailed, than the nonstudents' perceptions.

The students' fathers also were more likely to have highly skilled manual occupations, such as machinist, electrician, and carpenter, than were the nonstudents' fathers. Generally, the students' fathers were much more likely to be situated in the upper levels of the working class than the nonstudents' fathers. Overall, the students' fathers had higher average occupational prestige scores (based on the Hodge-Siegel-Rossi Prestige Scores) than the nonstudents' fathers (Davis and Smith 1988). The students' mothers, like the students' fathers, were more likely to have higher status occupations than the nonstudents' mothers. The six highest ranked occupational positions (based on prestige scales) among the respondents' mothers all were held by students' mothers.

Fathers were the principal breadwinners in most of the respondents' families. This conclusion is based upon the fathers' greater work longevity, greater length of tenure with one employer, and apparently higher paying occupations, in most cases. There were a few notable exceptions to this generalization. The mothers of the respondents typically performed roles in the home that facilitated the fathers being the principal breadwinners in most of these working class families. Despite the fact that 75% of the students' mothers were employed outside the home, 87.5% of the students' mothers also did all or most of the domestic housework. Similarly, although the majority (67%) of the nonstudents' mothers were employed outside the home, 92% of them also did most or all of the domestic housework.

The significance and importance of the mothers' earnings and financial contributions to many of the students' families should not be underestimated, however. Several students said that their mothers worked to help pay for their college tuition, and/or for their books, and/or for parochial school educations. In one college student's family, the mother worked in a factory to help enable the father to eventually complete his college education!

The students generally knew what their parents did for a living. In addition, they typically understood how their parents earned a living, what they experienced at work, and how it affected them. The students' parents often discussed their work in some detail with their children. Many students saw that their parents struggled and endured, and did not thrive. Students also recognized that their parents often had few choices. Parents often came home exhausted and drained. Unless the blue collar worker experiences some upward mobility, there is little hope of escape from this fate.

Several of the many college students' fathers who valued education took their sons to work with them. One father who was a sheet metal worker brought his son to work with him one day, to do air conditioning duct work. The son, a college student, described his experiences:

> *I busted my ass. My father said, "See, this is what it's like to break your back. How do you feel?" He asked me this at the end of the day. I said: "Tired." Then, he said: "If you go to school, you won't have to do this." I think he worked my ass off on purpose, but that was it. I only worked with him one day. I'll tell ya, though, I got a real taste of what it must be like for **him**.*

Like the students, the nonstudents generally were aware of what their parents did for a living. They also were aware, in a general sense, that work often was a struggle. Many of the nonstudents said that their parents did not talk about work very much, however. Thus, their knowledge and understanding of the details of parents' work experiences and struggles were more limited than was the case among the students.

Students' fathers often began their adult working lives working in lower skilled manual positions, and became foremen or supervisors in the same field. Examples include: several laborers or drivers, each of whom became a foreman; two fire fighters and three police officers, each of whom rose from fire fighter or patrolman to higher ranking officer or detective; and several assemblers or machine operators, each of whom became a line or production supervisor. Unlike the students' fathers, the nonstudents' fathers usually were not upwardly mobile.

LESSONS LEARNED

The college students often said that their fathers' job satisfaction and income levels rose after they were promoted. Thus, the students often saw that upward mobility was possible, and that upward mobility could lead to increased job satisfaction and monetary rewards. Students' comments consistently indicated that their parents wanted them to be upwardly mobile, since the parents consistently encouraged students to strive to attain better positions than they themselves had attained.

The college students' parents encouraged their children to be upwardly mobile for several reasons. First, the parents wanted their children to be financially more secure and more stable than they themselves had been. Second, they wished that their children could avoid the physical and emotional tolls of manual work. Third, they hoped that their children could attain higher status positions in the work world than they themselves had held.

The college students said that their parents often spoke of their own struggles as experiences that their children should strive to avoid. Students typically did listen to and understand the significance of this message from their parents. In addition, students often said that this was one motivating force in their own lives. One student's father simply told him: "You don't want to have to struggle like me." This student's father, like many other students' parents, saw education as the key to avoiding "the struggle."

This struggle was multifaceted. First and foremost, there was the economic uncertainty that permeated the lives of many of these families. Many of the respondents, both students and nonstudents, tersely summarized their plight by saying that "money was tight." A second aspect of the struggle was the physical demands of hard work. Parents often came home tired and spent. A third component involved frustrations stemming from the physical and financial challenges of both working class job and working class life. Some college students' parents also felt that they could have done more with their lives, and hoped that their children would do more than they had, several college students told me.

College students frequently said that they did not want to struggle like their parents did. College students often stated that their desire to attend college came, in part, from their wish to **avoid** some of that struggle. This college student's comments about his own career aspirations typify the feelings of many of the college students.

I don't want to end up like my father. I don't want to struggle like we did. I want to be comfortable.

College students often reported that their parents linked a college education with financial success and security. One college student's comments echoed those sentiments:

My father told me that I had to go to college, and then, and only then, would I be sure to earn a good living.

Another college student's comments were typical of the college students:

My father always said that you would never amount to much without an education. My mother also thought it was impor- tant. They both wanted us to do well in school.

To many of the college students' parents, not "amounting to much" meant that their children would end up in positions like their own. The students' parents clearly saw a college education as the means through which their children could "amount to something." Another college student said:

My father said that going to college gives you a choice. Then, you can do other things.

The "other things" to which this father referred would not require the manual toil that he himself endured.

One college student said that her father felt that, at work, he was "passed over" for promotions several times, in favor of "college kids" who knew much less than he did, but "had pieces of paper." He made it very clear to his daughter that, in order for her to be able to move up, she had to have a college degree. Generally, both the college stu- dents and their parents were keenly aware that the "piece of paper" (a four year college degree) was critically important to "moving up in the world."

The college students also saw that, by earning college degrees, they would increase their own range of choices. One student spoke of the choices in these terms:

> *I think it would be great, (paused) I would love to get up (for work), and, instead of saying I hate my job, this is great! I'm glad I'm going to work. I love what I do!*

Another college student spoke for many others, when she said:

> *I want to get a good job. I want to have a future. If you don't have an education today, you don't have much of a future.*

Occasionally, I sensed that some college students' parents were themselves frustrated, because they did not pursue a college education themselves. One student's comments about his mother are noteworthy:

> *My mother is really smart. She's a genius! She could've gone to any college she wanted. She did really good in school, and she could've gone on a scholarship. She got married instead. I guess that's what people did in those days.*

To this college student, "what people did" differed from what he did: attend college. Obviously, he felt that people should go to college, in his day.

Despite their much higher rates of upward mobility, compared to the nonstudents' fathers, the college students' fathers' experiences of upward mobility usually did not remove them from the working class. They emphasized education in general, and earning a college degree, in particular, for their children, so that their children might escape from manual work.

The aspirations the nonstudents' parents had for the nonstudents usually were limited. None of the nonstudents ever said anything indicating that their parents thought that their children could achieve upward mobility. The nonstudents were not encouraged to reach up; they more typically were encouraged to accept their lot in life. Many of the nonstudents' parents stressed "getting a job" or "earning a living," *instead of* an education. Two nonstudents' comments are representative.

My father stressed going to work, earning a living, getting a job.

My parents pushed me to get a civil service job, or a skilled trade.

The second nonstudent's comment suggests that upward mobility within the working class was the ultimate goal, not "escaping" the working class by earning a college degree.

Some of the nonstudents said that their parents wanted them to finish high school. That was the highest educational aspiration any of the nonstudents' parents had for the nonstudents, with one exception. In addition, some nonstudents expressed negative feelings about themselves.

Since education rarely was emphasized by their parents, and their parents usually were not openly communicative, the nonstudents did not learn of alternatives to working class jobs from their parents. Their fate was that they likely would struggle in working class jobs as their parents had done. The nonstudents themselves saw work as an inevitable struggle. A working class fatalism seemed to permeate these families. Instead of dreaming of "beating the odds," the nonstudents simply would follow in their parents' footsteps: they would "get jobs."

From the Life Stories research, it is clear that the parental influences were considerable. The college students' parents clearly influenced their children to attend college, and the nonstudents' parents clearly encouraged their children to get manual jobs, and "accept their lot in life."

8

SIBLINGS, OTHER RELATIVES, AND FRIENDS

The preceding discussion about parental influences leaves un-answered questions about siblings, other relatives, and friends. These influences are the subject of this chapter. As we will see, what a child's siblings do or do not do, pertaining to educational aspirations, often directly affects whether or not that child eventually will attend college. The oldest child, in particular, is especially important in influencing younger siblings. Other relatives have some effect on educational aspirations, but older siblings' influences are far more significant and important. Finally, friends are influential, but their influences often augment and parallel the influences of parents and older siblings.

SIBLINGS

In addition to looking to parents for guidance, young children often look up to older siblings. Children often admire and/or emulate their older sisters or brothers. Concerning homework, some college students said that they were helped with their homework by older siblings who eventually attended college. Whether or not such assistance took place, college student respondents often saw their older (college bound) siblings as significant role models who influenced them to aspire to attend college. The influences of these older siblings typically augmented the influences of their parents.

Older siblings who attended college could serve as "modelers" (Cohen 1987) for younger siblings. They could speak about college from their own personal experiences, whereas their working class parents who did not attend college themselves could not. College students who had older siblings who also attended college often did speak to those siblings about college. The college students frequently reminded me during the interviews, however, that their parents typically were the most influential people in their lives concerning valuation of education. This occurred at various points throughout the interviews, and most noticeably at the conclusion of many interviews.

Most of the college students had at least one sibling of college age (18 or older) at the time of the interview. An interesting pattern was common within these families. In 65% of the college students' families, **all** college age siblings (55 out of 55) still were attending or had attended college! This supports my feeling that college attendance might "run in certain families." The data also suggests that, within the families of the college students, birth order factors do not seem to correlate strongly with college attendance. What all siblings in each nuclear family have in common are their **parents**. It also is possible that, since the first borns usually did attend college, they set a positive example which the younger siblings then followed.

LAUNCHING "THE PIONEERS"

Approximately 25% of the college students interviewed were the first children in their respective families to attend college. I call these college students "the pioneers." The pioneers were extremely likely to focus on open communication with their parents when discussing their familial relationships. All but one of the pioneers stated that this was the essence of their relationships with their respective parents.

Open communication within working class families correlates strongly with launching pioneers. Furthermore, open communication between parents and children seems to be important for first borns, if they are to attend college. Parents of pioneers effectively are trying to alter the established pattern within their families pertaining to college attendance. Open communication helps facilitate this transformation. Once a new pattern has been initiated (someone, the pioneer, now does attend college), new social forces are operating to further encourage younger siblings to attend college as well. They can now emulate their older siblings, and, like them, attend college.

The pioneers can reinforce their parents' influences, and emphasize education to their younger sisters and brothers. Pioneers also are able to serve as modelers (Cohen 1987), a role that their non-college educated parents cannot fill completely, although some may have filled it partially by reading. By serving as "modelers," the pioneers augment the parents' roles as "definers" (Cohen 1987).

Several other findings, discussed previously, are pertinent to this discussion. Excluding respondents who were first borns, the oldest children within the college students' nuclear families were most likely to attend college. The large majority of the college students' siblings, excluding first borns, also attended college. The most common pattern, in fact, was that all of the college age siblings of the college students attended college, with this pattern occurring in fully two thirds of these families.

These data, in conjunction with the findings pertinent to pioneers, suggest a more general conclusion. The process of producing working class children who aspire to attend college occurs, to a significant degree, within the nuclear family. Some working class families seem to produce children, most or all of whom will attend college. Other working class families seem to produce children, most of whom will not attend college. Non-nuclear relatives and friends typically augment these nuclear family influences.

NON-NUCLEAR RELATIVES AND COLLEGE ASPIRATIONS

Occasionally, a cousin who did attend college did influence a college student to attend college, but this occurred infrequently. Each college student who spoke of a cousin's influence spoke of that cousin as someone with whom she/he had a close relationship. These cousins were seen frequently, and they had a strong influence on each college student's desire to attend college. One student, typical of the others, called his only college student cousin his "best friend," and saw him "constantly."

Several college students who discussed their cousins informed me that most or all of the children of "certain" aunts and uncles did attend college, and that most of the children of other aunts and uncles did not attend college. College attendance among the cousins also seemd to run in certain nuclear families.

One aunt and one cousin were seen as very significant others by one college student. Both attended college, and became nurses. The college student told me: "I really admired them. I think they were the reason why I thought I wanted to be a nurse." Another student said that his great uncle "always had a lot of books," and always told him how important education was. This description of a non-nuclear relative sounds like the descriptions many students offered of their parents. These two college students, like many others, reminded me that their non-nuclear relatives' influences were in addition to their parents' influences, and not as important as their parents' influences.

One college student said of two of his uncles, both college educated, and both fairly close to his age, that they "were like two older brothers" to him, and he saw them frequently. These two uncles both are professionals (one, an engineer; the other, a medical doctor), and both constantly stressed education to the college student, as did his parents. He also saw that both uncles struggled less than his father did, and earned higher incomes. In this case, these two uncles' influences pertaining to education may have been even more important than the student's parents' influences. His parents stressed education in general; his uncles helped him find a specific focus. Due in part to his uncles' influences, this student "always loved science," majored in biology, and planned to become a medical doctor or a chiropractor.

Some college students spoke of the influences of non-nuclear relatives who did not attend college, but still influenced them to aspire to go. One such college student, typical of others, said that his uncles and cousins were very important people in his life, and that they stressed college for him. Most of his uncles and cousins were laborers or construction workers.

One college student in particular was very conscious of her role as what I have called "the pioneer" in her family. She told me that she took her newfound role very seriously, since her younger cousins looked up to her. To her, her role included doing as well as she could do in school, and talking to her younger cousins about school. She hoped that, by setting a good and successful example, her younger cousins would emulate her, and attend college themselves. Among the college students who did have one or a few college graduates in their families, many emulated those college graduates. The pioneer in each family may play a particularly important role.

These data suggest that when cousins or other non-nuclear college educated kin are close relatives who are seen frequently, they may have considerable influence on the educational aspirations of working class children. These non-nuclear influences usually augmented and reinforced rather than superseded the nuclear family influences, both according to the college students themselves, and based on my assessment of other social research.

ADULT ACQUAINTANCES' INFLUENCES

Several college students said that acquaintances who were not peers or close friends influenced them to aspire to attend college. One college student said that her family doctor talked to her about college. He told her: "They can take away your arm or your leg, but they can't take away your brain." She continued. "I was really impressed by him. I admired him." She also said that a coworker "pushed me to go to college, and I pushed her." Another student became friendly with a few scientists at his place of employment, Brookhaven National Laboratory, and they suggested that he attend college. In general, however, the college student respondents were much more likely to have close friends, rather than casual friends or adult acquaintances, encourage them to aspire to attend college.

PEER INFLUENCES

Peers also are important in most young Americans' lives. I raised several questions about the influence of peers in the Life Stories research.

Did the college students' peers value education, as their parents generally did? Did the nonstudents' peers value education, or did they generally not value education, like the nonstudents' parents? Were college aspirations (and future attendance) typical or atypical, among each group of friends? Did peers talk with the respondents about attending college or not? Did peers do their schoolwork and encourage respondents to do their schoolwork, or not? Did the respondents behave as their friends did in these matters, or not?

The peers who are closest to each respondent likely will have the most significant effects on that respondent. Thus, the effects of close friends, best friends, and serious girlfriends or boyfriends likely will be more important than the effects of casual friends or acquaintances. The college student respondents' close friends were compared to the nonstudent respondents' close friends and any differences analyzed.

Most of the college students said that someone other than their parents had stressed the importance of education in general, and/or a college education in particular to them. Some of these people were friends or acquaintances. In sharp contrast, among the nonstudents, this was rare. Very few of the nonstudents said that someone else, besides parents, had talked about college or stressed education; nearly all said that no one else had.

CHOOSING FRIENDS: PROXIMITY AND VALUES

The process of choosing neighborhood friends and acquaintances is constrained in large part by neighborhood characteristics. Working class children in cities and suburbs often live in working class neighborhoods, and thus typically come in contact primarily with other working class children living in their neighborhoods. Since the large majority of working class children will not attend college, most working class children do not live near many children who will be attending college. If peer associations and influences are important to college aspirations, then the future college attenders must develop peer associations that will not conform to this most common pattern.

Suburban residential patterns often limit the choices of friends for young children, because they generally will not come in contact with a very large number of children, given spatial dispersion. As they get older, and they attend a high school from a larger geographical area, they will come in contact with a much larger number of children than they met in their local neighborhoods. Some of these children may not be working class, although it is likely that many will be. Furthermore, given a much larger group from which to choose, working class children are more likely to meet (and possibly befriend) several or more college bound working class children in their high schools.

Although a few of the college students spoke of some friends whose families were more affluent than their own, I was not able to ascertain systematically the class backgrounds of the respondents' friends in general. To my knowledge, based on what the respondents told me, the respondents' conceptions of the class backgrounds of their friends typically was limited to the degree of affluence of their friends' families. The respondents rarely said anything to me that indicated that they were keenly aware of the occupational and educational characteristics of their friends' parents.

FRIENDS, CROWDS, AND EDUCATION

The majority of the college students said that "all" or "almost all" or "most" or "many" of their friends growing up eventually attended college. This contrasts sharply with the nonstudents, only 8% of whom said the same about their friends. The large majority of the nonstudents (83%) said that "a few" or "one" or "none" of their friends growing up eventually attended college.

By asking respondents to describe the crowds they "hung out with" growing up, I encouraged them to think of the peers with whom they associated as a group, although friends likely would be included within the crowd. I also could double-check data obtained from the respondents pertaining to friends and college attendance against their descriptions of their respective crowds. The "friends" and the "crowds" generally had similar attitudes about education.

The large majority of the college students described their respective crowds as "college bound" and/or "good students" and/or "nerds." Although there is no guarantee that such people all were college bound, many of the (future) college students did regularly associate with peers who generally were academically oriented, and often were not members of the "in crowd" growing up. Several college students defined "nerd" as "studious" or "college bound." The college student respondents often seem to fit, in the words of one of the respondents, into an "academic oriented, good, wholesome type of crowd."

The in crowd typically consisted of young people who were popular and "cool." Being "cool" often meant being fashion conscious, being aware of the latest trends in popular music, and being desirable by many as a dating partner. Alcohol and/or other drugs often were a component of "having fun" in the in crowd. The in crowd typically was not academically oriented, and the high school was viewed primarily as a social setting by the in crowd.

Many college students discussed the important influences of friends or of their crowd in general, concerning education, at various times throughout the interview. College students often spoke of friends who themselves valued education highly, and were academically oriented. Two college students' comments are noteworthy.

All of my friends were high achievers, and I guess we all always felt like we all would go to college.

My friends (were the reason I went to college). All of my close friends (stressed education). We all studied together, and helped each other out with schoolwork.

Among the college students, friends sometimes "pushed" one another to succeed academically. One student, expressing these sentiments, said that he and his friends were "on top of each other" to do well in school. He said throughout the interview that his friends were an important influence on him. Sometimes they competed against one another:

All of my friends (were a major reason why this respondent went to college). We all were very competitive (concerning school). We were all in honors classes. I guess we always knew we were all going to college.

Most of the college student respondents said that they were in crowds that avoided "trouble." Trouble was defined by the college students as including drug and/or alcohol use, serious juvenile delinquency, and/or trouble in school. Drug use typically pertained to marijuana, although occasionally other hard drugs were mentioned. Avoiding trouble may be a significant factor, if a working class child is to aspire to attend college. The students were much more likely to speak negatively of crowds that were in trouble, when discussing their own crowds. One student said:

(My crowd was) Definitely not the dirt bags or burnouts. Not the druggies.

To the college students, "druggies" or "burnouts" were people who used drugs more than occasionally.

In some cases, the college students' friends were influential in encouraging the college student to avoid trouble:

If I had gotten into drugs, my friends would have been on top of me.

This student also said that he and his friends generally steered clear of "the dirt bags."

None of the nonstudents described their crowds growing up as "college bound" or "nerds" or "good students." In fact, the only two nonstudents who referred to their crowd in academic terms said "not the smart kids." In general, the lack of academic descriptions of their crowds indicates that the nonstudent respondents were not oriented towards school and schoolwork to anywhere near the same degree as the college student respondents were. These data suggest that school experiences may be another relevant aspect of the respondents' lives that may relate to whether or not they eventually attended college.

IN GROUPS, OUT GROUPS, AND "NERDS"

According to the respondents' own assessments, the college student respondents were more likely to be in groups in high school that other students labeled negatively than the nonstudents were. Among the college students, 40% said that they were "not popular" or "in an out group" or "nerds" or "loners," and only 8% of the nonstudents said the same.

There were several reasons why a significant percentage of the college students were not popular with other students. They were unpopular because they were "good" students, were college bound, got along well with teachers, were in advanced or accelerated classes, and/or were "nerds." Their academic orientation typically resulted in studying and learning taking precedence over fun and recreational pursuits.

To many of the college students, being popular in high school was not important. Speaking for others, one college student said that she "didn't care" what most other high school students said. She described her small crowd as: "a cross between the school band, and the bookworms or nerds." She had her small group of friends, but her group was not popular.

In general, a number of the college students used the term "nerd" or the like to identify themselves and/or their high school friends. They applied the negative label to themselves, and other students applied it to them. Generally, this label refers to students who were studious, academically oriented, not in the "in" or popular crowd, and who were "not into cliques." This type of student was not popular, and was negatively stereotyped in many of the college students' high schools.

One college student called her crowd: "The nerdy college bound crowd." Another college student described himself as a "dexter." (This is a reference to a cartoon character, "Poindexter," who was very studious, introspective, and cerebral). Most of his friends were "smart, in academic tracks, and liked fooling around with computers." He often was an "outcast" in school, because of his and his friends' academic orientation. Another college student summed up these feelings and experiences, expressed by numerous other college students:

We definitely weren't in the in crowd. (laughed) Some of those guys used to make fun of us, but I don't think any of them

*amounted to anything. I guess we were the clique who weren't
in any of the cliques.*

College students often used negative labels in describing their
own crowds. They usually accepted the status hierarchy of their high
schools, and typically did not aspire to become members of the higher
status group, commonly called the "in crowd." Those college student
respondents who were labeled "nerds" typically accepted the negative
label, but still wanted to be nerds.

The allure of the "in crowd" sometimes was attractive. One college student said that he was with the "in crowd" and "the jocks" early
in high school. "I didn't do as well in school as I should have, until
I left that crowd, and went on my own." This college student generally had been in advanced classes, but had not applied himself very
much until he left those crowds. He didn't do well in school when he
was in those crowds in part because doing well in school was not part
of the value system of those crowds. He chose acceptance in those
crowds and their value system, but only temporarily. When he went
on his own, his parents, who wanted him to leave the in crowd, were
pleased. Since pleasing his parents was important to this college student, he eventually was pleased as well.

The experiences of another college student reflect the orientation
of the college students in general. She participated in a foreign exchange program, spending most of her senior year in high school in
a remote region of the Philippines. Other students said to her: "How
can you miss your senior year?" These other students, most of whom
were not college bound, were referring to "the fun" of being a senior. She felt that the exchange would be "an incredible learning and
growth experience," and she wanted to learn and grow.

Another college student's comments further illustrate that the cerebral pursuits of the college student respondents contributed to their
unpopularity.

*I wasn't really popular. I had a few close friends. My friends
and I were deeper. We liked to get into these deep philosophi-
cal discussions. Most of the other kids were so superficial. We
were different.*

Like many of the college students, this college student had a small circle of friends, most of whom were college bound.

TWO DIFFERENT CROWDS

Many of the college students discussed two different and distinct crowds. None of the nonstudents did. One college student said that she had "a few Jewish friends," and they went to college. She said that their parents always emphasized learning, and:

> *laid the guilt trip on their kids. There was never any doubt. They were expected to go to college. That impressed me. I always admired them for that.*

She also said that most of her friends did not attend college, but that those friends were very different from the college bound friends she "always admired." Those friends who did not attend college were not academically oriented, and had no college aspirations.

Most of the college students said that they had "school friends" (from high school), and "neighborhood" friends. Their school friends usually attended college and their neighborhood friends often did not attend college. For most of the college students, their school (and college bound) friends were much more important, and more significant.

How did the college students find and befriend other college bound students when they all were in high school? For some of the college students, tracking into advanced or accelerated classes facilitated their meeting other academically oriented students. Other college students told me that they met these friends in activities or clubs, such as the school band, chorus, and honor society. Other college students did not specify how they befriended and were befriended by other college bound high school students.

BEST FRIENDS, CLOSE FRIENDS, BOYFRIENDS, AND GIRLFRIENDS

In the interviews, respondents were asked to discuss their "best" or "closest" friends. Nearly all of the college students had one or more best friends or closest friends who attended college. Of all the best or closest friends discussed by the college students, 84% of them attended college.

Significantly, only 4 of the 48 college students did not have at least one "best" or "closest" friend who attended college.

Many of the college students spoke of close friends as if they were family. They saw one another very often, shared common values, and shared the same aspiration: to attend college. The college students often had open communication with their close friends. This facilitated problem solving and crisis resolution through emotional support and encouragement. In general, these friendships strongly resembled the relationships that the college students had with their parents. In addition, the close friends, who valued education as the college students' parents did, helped to reinforce those values. This relates to college aspirations.

Only 10 of the 24 nonstudents interviewed had a "best" or "closest" friend who attended college. Most of these nonstudents, however, each said that most of their friends did not attend college.

Similar to the pattern found among best and closest friends, the large majority of the college students' serious girlfriends or boyfriends also attended college. Once again, this contrasts sharply with what the nonstudents told me during the interviews. The vast majority of the nonstudents reported that their serious girlfriends or boyfriends did not attend college.

When a boyfriend or girlfriend of a college student did not value education, the relationship itself became precarious. One college student, a man, said that his first serious girlfriend from high school did not attend college. During the interview, he said: "I tried to straighten her out, push her in the right direction" (to college). He was unsuccessful, and he ended their relationship. A second college student, a woman, broke up with her first serious boyfriend over her college attendance. He never attended college, and he wanted her to quit.

I conclude that a working class child in a peer group, most of whose members are college bound, is likely to attend college. She or he also is fairly likely to have or find a serious boyfriend or girlfriend in high school who also is college bound. Within the college bound peer group, the college bound boyfriend or girlfriend reinforces the group's tendencies: for its members to attend college. Additionally, it is important to the college bound working class adolescent that a serious boyfriend or girlfriend also is college bound.

A working class adolescent in a different peer group, with few college bound children, is much less likely to have or find a serious girlfriend or boyfriend who is college bound. It also seems to be much less important, to such teens, that a serious girlfriend or boyfriend is college bound. Similarly, that adolescent also is less likely to attend college.

9

SCHOOL EXPERIENCES

Research strongly suggests that early academic success is a strong predictor of future academic success (See, for example: Jencks, et al 1972; Persell 1977; Oakes 1985). In the case of working class children, do their earlier school experiences influence whether or not they plan to attend college?

I investigated the earlier school experiences of both the college students and the nonstudents. Comments made by the respondents suggested that an investigation of school experiences might be fruitful. When discussing their peers, the college students often referred to two groups of friends: one in the neighborhood, and the other, qualitatively different, at school. This indicated that school experiences or influences might differ in some significant ways from neighborhood experiences and influences. Since none of the nonstudent respondents mentioned two different groups of friends, I thought that their friends at school might be similar to their friends in the neighborhood. Another possibility is that the neighborhood, not the school, was their primary focal point. So, an investigation and analysis of the nonstudent respondents' school experiences also seemed warranted.

Did the working class college student respondents generally have positive experiences and academic success through high school? If yes, did these earlier positive school experiences encourage them to attend college? Similarly, did the working class nonstudent respondents generally have fewer positive experiences and less academic success through high school than the college student respondents? If yes, did their high school experiences discourage them from attending college? Did the college student respondents and the nonstudent respondents have significantly different experiences in high school? Did the high school experiences of the college student respondents reinforce and support the pro education messages they generally received from their parents and peers? Did the nonstudents have experiences in high school that reinforced the messages they received from their parents and peers: do not aspire to attend college? Finally, several college students had referred to teachers or counselors as important significant others even before the interviews turned to a discussion of school experiences. None of the nonstudents mentioned teachers or counselors during the earlier part of the interviews. This suggested that the college students' school experiences through high school might differ qualitatively from the school experiences of the nonstudents, and were worthy of investigation.

HOW DID RESPONDENTS DO ACADEMICALLY IN HIGH SCHOOL?

The college students and the nonstudents saw themselves in very different lights academically. Most of the college students, but none of the nonstudents, said that they usually did "well" or "very well" in school. Similarly, none of the college students, but one third of the nonstudents, said that they "had problems" in at least some classes.

Please recall that most of the college students, but only one of the nonstudents reported that both parents "pushed" or "stressed" or "emphasized" or "valued" education, or thought that education was "very important" or "important." College attendance for the college students typically correlated with both parental valuation of education and doing well academically before college. Nonattendance typically correlated with both lack of parental valuation of education and not having done well in school for the nonstudent respondents.

Approximately one third of the college students, but none of the nonstudents, were in at least some advanced or accelerated classes while in high school. The nonstudents were much less likely than the college students to have been in college bound tracks in high school. None of the college students, but one third of the nonstudents said that they were "not in an academic track."

In sum, the college students were much more likely to be positively tracked in high school than the nonstudents. The nonstudents were much more likely to be negatively tracked than the college students. What factors affect track placement?

Persell (1977:89), upon reviewing an extensive number of studies, stated:

In brief, standardized test scores, teachers' recommendations, and pupils' social class and race are related to track placement. Tests and teacher recommendations themselves appear to be related to race and class.

Oakes (1985:51), from her study of tracking in 25 schools, concludes that:

The locus of control regarding track decisions at most of the schools resided with the counselors. Teachers appear to have had a considerable say at many schools, parents at a few, and students at almost none.

HOW DID RESPONDENTS FEEL ABOUT SCHOOL?

Given that the college students usually had academic success, and that their parents generally valued education, it is perhaps not surprising that only one college student "didn't like school" (before college). She also was the only college student who had dropped out of high school. The majority of the nonstudents "didn't like school." Of all comments about school made by the nonstudents, 90% were negative. Since the nonstudents' parents typically did not value education, and the nonstudents did not do well academically, negative feelings about school among the nonstudents are not surprising.

The social class of the college student respondents sometimes was a factor contributing to how they reported they were treated by other students and by teachers. One college student described her (public) high school as "a blue collar high school," and said that the teachers and administrators "were not nice, especially to the blue collar kids." She plans to become a university professor. I suspect that, as a professor, she will not do to blue collar students what some teachers have done to countless blue collar students in this society throughout its history.

COLLEGE STUDENT RESPONDENTS' EXPERIENCES WITH TEACHERS IN HIGH SCHOOL

Teachers generally are major agents of socialization in American schools. The teacher typically is the authority figure in the classroom, and has major inputs into student evaluation. Teachers also have significant input into tracking decisions (Persell 1977; Oakes 1985). For these reasons, any investigation of the respondents' school experiences must address their relationships with their teachers.

The respondents' teachers had significantly more formal education than nearly all of the respondents' parents. The college students themselves also are likely to surpass their parents' educational attainments. For the upwardly mobile working class child, then, teachers' influences may be particularly significant, especially as modelers (Cohen 1987). Most of the college students described their experiences with teachers before college as generally good and positive, with a significant percentage speaking in very positive terms.

Overall, the college students were much more likely to have had mostly positive experiences with teachers than with other students through high school. This may be significant. Many of the students looked up to or admired at least some of their teachers. The teachers of the college students often encouraged them. The college students often emphasized the positive importance of teachers being "down to earth." Negative experiences, without some positive experiences to counterbalance them, were rare among the college students. Most of the negative comments about teachers concerned "stuck up" and "aloof" teachers. Teachers being accessible to and personable with working class students appear to be factors that encourage such children to aspire to attend college.

NONSTUDENT RESPONDENTS' EXPERIENCES WITH TEACHERS IN HIGH SCHOOL

For the nonstudent respondents to aspire to attend college, their parents' typically negative or neutral feelings about education had to be counteracted in some way. Teachers might provide such positive feelings about education. For this positive message to be received, the nonstudent respondents would have to have had positive feelings about their teachers. Unfortunately, only 25% of the nonstudents said that they generally had such good or positive experiences with teachers.

Based on their accounts, what generally were lacking in the nonstudents' experiences in high school were adults attempting to orient them towards aspiring to attend college. Nearly all of the nonstudent respondents said that no adults beyond their nuclear families ever spoke to them about attending college. Half of the nonstudent respondents said that they usually had negative experiences with teachers through high school. Many of the others had "mixed" or "so-so" experiences with teachers. Negative or mixed experiences with teachers, given the nonstudents respondents' general orientation away from education, hardly seem to be enough to encourage them to aspire to attend college.

COLLEGE EXPERIENCES OF COLLEGE STUDENT RESPONDENTS

A large percentage of college attenders in the United States drop out, especially among students from poor or working class families (Astin et al. 1988; Astin 1975). The college experiences of the college students in the Life Stories research therefore may be important. Their experiences while attending college may give us glimpses of how and why they remained in college, and may give us clues as to why some working class college attenders drop out.

Most of the college students began to attend college immediately after high school, at age 17 or 18. For most of the college students, beginning college was not unlike continuing their schooling into the next grade. Thus, there was continuity without interruption in their educational experiences. Most of the college students generally said that they "liked" or "enjoyed" college. These findings are consistent with the mostly positive experiences that these respondents said they had in school before college.

Most college students, not surprisingly, expressed at least one comment or complaint in discussing their college experiences. The most common complaint was that they "disliked" or "hated" large classes, with one third responding in that manner. Some specifically stated that they "liked" or "preferred" smaller classes.

Another complaint expressed by 25% of the college students was that they felt that professors often were "aloof," "stuck up," "uncaring," and/or "unavailable" or "unwilling" to help students with questions or problems. One college student told me that he had an ongoing problem with professors. He said that he "hated the attitudes" of most professors. Twenty per cent of the college students specifically said that they felt "lost" or "scared" or "intimidated" at college, usually because of large classes, aloof professors, or both.

Several college students spoke during the interviews of denigration of working class people at the university. The comments of one college student, who, at the time, was a graduate student, are similar to what other college students described and experienced. In an undergraduate course, the college student told me, an English professor was telling a story, using an analogy. The professor said that "blue collar people, people who work with their backs, have **only** their backs, and are **too stupid** to do anything else." The respondent continued:

> *She really pissed me off! I argued with her in class, and after class, and it went back and forth. I wrote an essay for her, and she gave me an F! I don't think she ever even read it. I never got an F. I never failed anything! I'm not one to complain, but I knew!*

This professor apparently had little understanding of how it felt to be the child of working class parents forced to listen to such dribble. Such comments and attitudes are not uncommon. (See, for example, Ryan and Sackrey: 1984.) From a working class perspective, this professor might appear to be ignorant. This student then went to the department chair to protest:

> *I went to the department, and I said to the chairman: "Read this paper. Do you think it's an F?" After a while, I said to him: "Why am I wasting my time here with you?" I felt, you know, that professors protect each other. So, I went right to the dean, knocked on his door. I got a B in the course.*

Fortunately for this college student, he found an avenue for airing his grievance. I wonder how many other students, working class or otherwise, at every level of education, simply would have accepted both the "F," **and** the blame for it.

Demo and Savin-Williams (1983) found that an adolescent's level of academic skills is strongly predictive of her or his self image. Students who do well in school are more likely to have more positive self images. Snarey and Vaillant (1985) indicate that upwardly mobile working class children have more positive self images than other working class children.

Successful and upwardly mobile students, like the college students from my Life Stories research, seem to have developed stronger defenses against people who might talk down to them or put them down. The college students' reactions to and comments about "stuck up" teachers indicate that at least some of these working class college students possess this trait. By attending college, they have entered a world frequented by few of their working class peers. A strong ego defense for some may help them believe that they belong there.

For help, advice, and guidance, the college student respondents would be likely to turn to their professors. That is consistent with their patterns throughout school of gravitating towards teachers, with whom they typically had positive relationships. Their professors, then, potentially are one major link that working class college students may have with the white collar or professional world they aspire to enter. Some of the college students found their professors lacking as mentors, and voiced their displeasure. Teaching assistants seldom filled the void.

The importance of guidance was emphasized by one college student. He had one very positive experience with a professor at a community college, because the professor related to him as a person, answered his questions, and gave him help and advice. After earning his associate's degree, he transferred to the large, local state university. There, he felt that many professors were "aloof," and he missed the guidance he once had.

Some college students said that some other students were "spoiled" or "stuck up" or "had it too easy." A number of the working class college students at some point during the interview had expressed an awareness that "some college students have it easier than others." They noticed that some college students worked fewer hours, if they were employed at all, than they did. They also saw some college students with "fancy clothes" or "expensive cars" and the like. To the working class students, these other students did not earn what they had. One college student respondent thought that wealthier students were spoiled, and unaware of the struggles that others, including his own parents, had to endure. He told me that they were living in the clouds, removed from the realities of his world. Social class differences do persist at the university and beyond.

SCHEDULES AND WORK LOADS OF COLLEGE STUDENT RESPONDENTS

Nearly all of the college students described their schedules as "very hectic" or "hectic" or "very busy" or "busy" or "crazy." Most of the college students said that they never had enough time to do everything that they had to do or wanted to do.

More than half of the college students worked 20 or more hours per week when they were full time undergraduate students. This large subgroup worked an average of 27.4 hours per week, during the semesters! Overall, the large majority of the college students worked 15 or more hours per week, during semesters, while attending college full time as undergraduates. According to Astin et al. (1988), 40.2% of all new American college undergraduate freshmen in 1988, including those of working class origin, worked 16 or more hours per week.

Counselors and advisors follow a general rule of thumb concerning undergraduate students' work load. The rule is that full time college students, (that is, those who are taking 12 or more credits per semester), should not work more than 20 hours per week during semesters. The majority of the working class college students in my research apparently broke this rule of thumb.

Why do I believe that the implications of this finding are so significant? Several of the college students themselves expressed the consequences in this way: "There are only so many hours in a day!" Many of the students said that they felt at least a bit overwhelmed. Their schedules were so hectic that they simply resigned themselves to the fact that they never would have enough time to do everything.

Professionals and many others, of course, might say the same thing about their schedules. Professional people, however, already have reached professional positions and possessed the resultant higher status. These working class college students, however, were trying to **become** white collar or professional people. They had not yet reached the positions they hoped to reach. Thus, the possible consequences of "not having enough time" might be different for them than for professional people.

For most of the college students, time, or more accurately, *lack* of time, was a very significant factor in their lives as undergraduates. They always seemed to be working under time pressure, and sometimes, with severe time constraints. Pressure does encourage some students to prioritize, and to avoid procrastination as if it were a death sentence. How they overcame time constraints that threatened to prevent them from achieving their educational goals will be discussed shortly.

The consequences of lack of sufficient time are likely to vary for different types of working class college students. The "better" student may see her or his grade point average drop a bit, may take longer to graduate, and/or may live without a social life or enough sleep. For the "less successful" working class college student, the one "on the edge," perhaps one common response is to "do poorly" in college, and eventually drop out.

According to Astin (1975), the most common reasons college dropouts gave for leaving college were: "boredom with classes" (32%); "financial difficulties" (28%); and "marriage, pregnancy, or other family responsibilities" (23%). As family income levels rose, college dropout rates generally fell. Among all college attenders, the students from the poorest families (financially speaking) had the highest dropout rates (31%), and were twice as likely to drop out as students from upper middle income families (16%). Working 25 or more hours per week consistently increased college dropout rates. Having a job, but working less than 25 hours per week, decreased college dropout rates.

Social class background, which imposes time constraints, likely affects the success or failure of working class college students. These time constraints are caused in part by financial need.

COPING STRATEGIES OF COLLEGE STUDENT RESPONDENTS

How do working class college students cope, given their typically busy, often frantic schedules? The large majority of the college students said that they "prioritized" or the like. Most of the college students ordered the various tasks that they had to complete, and schoolwork typically was the first priority. Prioritizing is one coping strategy that generally is common among successful college students (Astin 1975). Given that the college students in my research worked more hours, on average, than college students nationwide (Astin et al. 1988), prioritizing was especially essential, if they were to be successful. Many of the college student respondents first learned to place schoolwork first among tasks on the list of priorities as children.

Another common thought, expressed by one third of the college students, was "I organize," or "I am well organized." Typically, the college students "always" were well organized. One aspect of this, discussed by several college students, was to "budget time well" and/ or "set up a schedule." Resiliency and determination also were important, and discussed often.

Another common theme expressed by 25% of the college students was: "didn't date much" or "didn't have much free time" or the like. Twenty per cent said that they "pruned" their schedules. The pruning typically pertained to activities unrelated to schoolwork. Even among the "lucky few" who consistently did find the time to go out, leisure pursuits did not take precedence over academic responsibilities.

Another common coping strategy, discussed by 25% of the college students, was to juggle. Family and other responsibilities sometimes were put aside, if only temporarily. Twenty per cent of the college students said that they "skip sleep" or "sleep less." One college student's comments on coping strategies express the sentiments of many: "I don't sleep much." These working class college students are sleeping less because there are not enough hours in the week to study, attend classes, work, **and** sleep. They are not losing sleep due to partying, and an active, full night life that, to them, often seem characteristic of some more affluent college students.

What do the various coping strategies, viewed together, tell us about the working class college student respondents? Like most of their parents, the college students did value and emphasize education. Many of these college students, again like many of their parents, were well organized. (The majority of the college students said that both parents were very well organized or well organized.) Most of the college students usually had done well in school, had ample parental and family support, and their families generally were strong, close, and intact. Like themselves, most of their siblings and close friends attend or have attended college. Finally, they see education as their first priority.

Certainly, individual factors (like work ethic and supportive families) help explain some of the successes and failures of working class students. Many working class children in the U.S. fail to attend college, however. This cannot be the "fault" of individualistic factors alone. Widespread inequalities in the United States, which help create unequal opportunities, help explain why so many less affluent children "fail."

PAYING FOR COLLEGE

Difficult financial circumstances were common to both the college student respondents and the nonstudent respondents. Therefore, financial status alone does not correlate with college attendance or nonattendance among the respondents. This most certainly does not imply that financial concerns were not paramount for many of the college student respondents and their families. Despite limited discretionary income many of the college students' parents helped their children finance their college educations.

The large majority of the college students received some financial assistance from their parents in meeting their college expenses or tuition. Thus, the working class college students in my Life Stories research were similar to college students in general, according to Astin et al. (1988). The large majority of the students also received some form of outside financial assistance: scholarships, loans, and/or financial aid. Nearly half of the college students reported having obtained loans, one third received scholarships, and nearly half received some other form of financial aid, all as undergraduates. (Multiple responses were possible.)

10

A SURVEY OF OTHER RESEARCH

How family life affects whether or not working class children attend college is a major focus of this book. Quite a bit of other research has investigated how and why some children plan to go to college, while others do not. Much of that research zeroes in on the family. Some of the research has looked at family differences among families of similar social class backgrounds. That research is especially relevant to our key purpose here.

FAMILY EXPERIENCES, VALUES, AND ACTIONS, AND THEIR EFFECTS

A significant amount of social research has shown that, if parents value and encourage education, children are more likely to succeed academically, and aspire to attend college (Sewell and Shah 1968; Conklin and Dailey 1981; Becher 1984; Carpenter and Fleishman 1987; Cohen 1987; Stage and Hossler 1989; Rutchick, Smyth, Lopoo, and Dusek 2009; Spera, Wentzel, and Matto 2009; Kirk, Lewis-Moss, Nilsen, and Colvin 2011). This effect is independent of income levels, which also had strong positive effects on college plans (Sewell and Shah 1968). Immigrant mothers' positive educational hopes for their children improved their children's grades in school (Henry, Merten,

Plunkett, and Sands 2008). Having parents who read encourages children to read, and reading frequently and at a young age helps children do well in school (Chomsky 1972; Anderson, et al. 1985; Dunn 1981). Reading early helps children develop their use of and understanding of language and vocabulary. This greatly improves their ability to do well in school in the early grades. In my Life Stories research, I found that doing well in school early on increases the likelihood that children will continue to do well academically and eventually attend college.

According to Cohen (1987), parents, as "definers," generally influence their children to strive for academic success by their expectations and attitudes toward education. As "modelers," parents exemplify college attenders or college graduates, and their children may emulate them and their behaviors (Cohen 1987). To Cohen, parents who value education define education as something that their children should strive for. These parents are likely to tell their children that education is important. They also may reward or praise their children for doing well in school, and may react negatively to their children not doing well in school. Parents who couldn't care less about education are telling their children that education is not important. Their behaviors, such as lack of interest in their children's schoolwork and academic performance, reflect their indifference about education.

Cohen found that, in the definer role, working class parents could be as effective as white collar or professional parents. Since most working class parents have not attended college, Cohen concluded that few could serve as modelers. Although these parents could not model attending college per se, I suggest that working class parents may serve as modelers by doing what successful college students, and professionals, often do: read. Such partial modeling may encourage working class children to aspire to attend college. In addition, older siblings who attend college also may serve as modelers. I found this to be the case in my Life Stories research.

Clark (1983) studied poor Black families living in public housing projects in Chicago. Each family had one senior high school student; half were in the top 20% of their classes academically, and half were in the bottom 20% of their classes. These families were observed in their homes for many hours, and their patterns of interaction were studied intensively.

Clark found that parental emphasis on education was much more common in the families with successful high school students. These parents took a strong interest in how their children did at school, and expected their children to work to succeed academically. They also were very concerned that the school fulfills its role in educating children. They met with teachers, visited the school, and became involved in various school activities. Clark states that, in their relationships with their children, the parents of the high achievers were openly communicative, nurturing, and supportive. They frequently interacted and conversed with their children. They also acted to insure that their children managed their time well and productively.

Parental indifference was typical in poor families with struggling high school students, according to Clark's research. These parents did not value education, and did not show a strong interest in how their children were doing academically. They rarely visited the school, except to respond to a negative report. They did not supervise their children to anywhere near the same degree as the parents of the high achievers did. Clark called the lower achievers' parents' style of parenting "unsponsored independence," in contrast with the high achievers' parents' style, which Clark described as "sponsored independence."

Another recent study of poorer children living in public housing followed Clark's research. Nebbitt, Lombe, LaPoint, and Bryant (2009) found that children who were more involved in family activities did better in school than children who were less involved in family activities. Parental involvement in their children's lives and "parenting quality" may be most important in the most difficult economic circumstances. In their research, Herbers, Cutuli, Lafavor, Vrieze, et al. (2011) found that "parenting quality" affected homeless children's academic performance. Positive high quality parenting also reduced the amount of risk for high risk children (Herbers, Cutuli, Lafavor, Vrieze, et al. 2011). Parental involvement in their children's lives improved children's performance in school in immigrants' families (Plunkett, Behnke, Sands, and Choi 2009). Immigrant mothers' educational hopes for their children affected their children's grades in school (Henry, Merten, Plunkett, and Sands 2008). Clearly, if poor parents, homeless parents, and immigrant parents all can have positive affects on their children's academic performance, you could have the same positive affects on your children's school work.

Henderson (1987), in an assessment of a growing body of research evidence, reported that children's academic achievements generally improved when parents become involved in positive ways in their children's education. I investigated this within working class families and also found this to be true.

In agreement with Clark and Henderson concerning parental involvement in school activities is Dornbusch (1986), who studied high school students and their families. Dornbusch found that whether or not parents attended school functions such as open school nights influenced their children's academic performance independent of parental income and education levels.

Dornbusch, et al. (1987) found that parenting style is a better predictor of student achievement than parents' education levels. Specifically, Dornbusch and his associates described three basic parenting styles: authoritarian, permissive, and authoritative (Dornbusch, et al., 1987:1245):

Authoritarian Parenting: Parents attempted to shape, control, and evaluate the behavior and attitudes of their children in accordance with an absolute set of standards; parents emphasize obedience, respect for authority, work, tradition, and the preservation of order; verbal give and take between parent and child is discouraged.

Permissive Parenting: Parents are tolerant and accepting toward the child's impulses, use as little punishment as possible, make few demands for mature behavior, and allow considerable self regulation by the child.

Authoritative Parenting: An expectation of mature behavior from the child and clear setting of standards by the parents; firm enforcement of rules and standards, using commands and sanctions when necessary; encouragement of the child's independence and individuality; open communication between parents and children, with encouragement of verbal give and take; and recognition of the rights of both parents and children.

Recent research continues to support the important work of Dornbusch and his colleagues. Blondal and Adalbjarnardottir (2009) concluded that authoritative parenting decreases children's dropout rates. Turner, Chandler, and Heffer (2009) found that authoritative parenting improves the academic performance of children who are attending college.

Holding parental education level constant, children of authoritative parents earned higher grades in high school than children of either permissive or authoritarian parents. In my Life Stories research, I found that most of the parents of the college students clearly were authoritative. Most of the nonstudents' parents were either authoritarian or permissive.

Kohn (1977), following others, concludes from his research that working class parents have a greater tendency towards authoritarian behaviors than do middle class parents. Kohn also found that middle class people are more self directed, and working class (blue collar) people are more conformist. More specifically, according to Kohn, middle class values include self direction, internal standards of behavior, intent of actions is more important than results or consequences of actions, and the spirit of the law is more important than the letter of the law. Thus, Kohn concludes that flexibility and permissiveness are more common among middle class parents than among working class parents.

Kohn leaves unanswered the question whether or not some working class parents value education strongly, while others do not. If such differences do exist, then they might help explain why some working class children do much better in school than others. I investigated this thread thoroughly in my Life Stories research. It is very clear from that research that working class parents who value education strongly are much more likely to have children who do well in school and eventually attend college. Working class parents who do not value education typically have children who do not do well in school and will not attend college.

In my Life Stories research, the college student respondents consistently spoke about the positive relationships that they had with their parents. They typically viewed these relationships as being more important than material things or lifestyle growing up. I have argued previously that these positive relationships with their parents help explain why the college student respondents had attended college. Several other recent studies support this conclusion. Orthner, Jones-Sanpei, Hair, and Moore, et al. (2009) found that positive parent-child relationships increase children's college attendance rates. Murray (2009) concluded that positive parent-child relationships improve children's school performance. Another recent study summarizes these findings: "If today there exists a single transcendent idea about the family-school connection, it is that a positive parent-child relationship improves children's chances of succeeding in school." (Lopez Turley, Desmond, and Bruch (2010).

WORK EXPERIENCES AND SELF IMAGE

Kohn (1977) related the difference in values between working class and middle class people to the contrasting work experiences of blue collar versus white collar workers. One key thesis of Kohn is "that class-correlated occupational conditions really do affect values, orientation, and psychological functioning" (Kohn 1977: xliii).

Sennett and Cobb (1972) argued that blue collar workers often have poor or self-limiting self images because of their work experiences. Because workers often are treated badly, and often with disrespect, by their "superiors," they are more likely to have a shaky self image. In addition, how American society in general denigrates and devalues blue collar workers does little to help improve the self conception of working people.

Rubin (1976) generally concurs with Sennett and Cobb. Rubin emphasizes the differences between what she terms the hourly blue collar workers, and the "lower middle class" of salaried office workers. Differences in overall work experiences between the two classes correlate with differences in self concept between the typical blue collar worker and the typical office worker.

The types of work experiences and life experiences one has can influence how one's self image develops. Sennett and Cobb's "hidden injuries" of class (Sennett and Cobb 1972) may be too generalized, however. They conclude that all of the working class people they studied had poor self images, and typically were self limiting. This seems a bit simplistic and unrealistic to me. There likely are qualitative and significant differences **within** the working class pertaining to self image. Such differences may relate to differences in work experiences and/or other factors. Differences in working class parents' self images may influence whether or not their children attend college. I conclude from my Life Stories research that this seems to be the case. Parents with positive self images and some upward mobility at work seemed to be more likely to encourage their children to aspire to attend college. Parents with poorer self images and little or no upward mobility at work seemed to be less likely to encourage their children to aspire to attend college.

According to Snarey and Vaillant (1985), upwardly mobile poor and working class children have more positive self images than do non-upwardly mobile children from similar backgrounds. The researchers concluded that positive self images help explain why some children of poor and working class parents attend college. Such children likely take criticism constructively, and believe in themselves and their abilities, even in the face of short-term failures. In working class language, they develop "a thick skin" or "a tough shell." Perseverance in school, and the achievement of long-term educational goals, results. These factors also were investigated in my Life Stories research, and I generally agree with Snarey and Vaillant.

UPWARD MOBILITY PATTERNS

According to my research findings, intergenerational mobility from lower working class to middle class seems likely to occur over more than two generations. Many of the students' parents and families in some significant ways were in the upper working class. They thus were positioned to launch their children to college, and likely future middle class status.

Fathers of the student respondents often were upwardly mobile; nonstudents' fathers rarely were. In addition, students often had at least one college educated older non-nuclear relative; nonstudents very rarely did. The college attenders, then, often had both definers, usually their parents, and modelers, at least one college educated older relative, in their families (Cohen 1987).

In some ways, the value system and behaviors of the students' parents more closely resemble middle class patterns rather than working class ones. The nonstudents' parents provide a stark contrast in these matters, more strongly resembling working class patterns.

Students' parents were more likely to read, a "hobby" more in line with middle class status. Students' parents typically valued and emphasized education, again more like middle class parents than working class parents. Nonstudents' parents typically did not value or emphasize education. Open communication, much more typical of the students' parents, and again resembling a middle class orientation, again contrasts with the nonstudents' parents.

The families of the student respondents generally could be characterized as being in the upper levels of the working class. The nonstudents' families, on the other hand, generally are more firmly situated within the heart of the working class. Their respective value systems correlate with these different statuses, and may affect one another. Values do not exist in a situational vacuum.

Values are influenced by the structural realities that people encounter. Upwardly mobile working class parents are more likely to see upward mobility for their children as possible, since upward mobility was possible for them. In addition, the employment prospects one faces likely affect how one views the world. During a period of economic growth and prosperity, parents might expect continued improvements for their children.

Less positive work experiences, in conjunction with lower rates of upward mobility, likely produce less optimism for the future. The nonstudents' parents generally were in lower status positions and experienced less upward mobility than the college students' parents. This sets the stage for lower expectations for their children.

Some readers might misinterpret the findings of this study pertaining to differences between the student respondents and their families, on the one hand, and the nonstudents and their families, on the other hand. The nonstudent respondents were similar to the students in some significant ways. I noted a strong work ethic among nearly all of the respondents, students and nonstudents alike. The same most certainly can be said of the nonstudents' parents, who, like the students' parents, worked very hard at their jobs and at home to try to support themselves and their children. The key differences between the two groups of respondents, as well as the key differences between the two groups of parents, lie elsewhere.

The nonstudents' parents' work experiences, less positive as they were than those of the students' parents, likely provided less justification for believing that life for themselves and their children would improve measurably in the future. With substantially lower upward mobility rates than the students' fathers, the nonstudents' fathers own experiences taught them that work was drudgery with little hope of qualitative improvement. They also saw that their wives were in similar circumstances.

The nonstudents' mothers often had lower status jobs than the students' mothers, and rarely experienced upward career mobility themselves. Thus, they also had work experiences that would encourage a more pessimistic assessment of their long term prospects for improvement. They found little solace in their husbands' work experiences.

Thus, within the nonstudents' families, both parents typically had work experiences that suppressed dreams of a better future for themselves and their children. Those few nonstudents' families in which a parent was upwardly mobile produced a disproportionately large number of the nonstudents' siblings who attended college. These findings suggest that parents' work experiences correlate with children's educational attainment levels within working class families.

In addition to work experiences, the early school experiences of their children affect parents' future expectations and behaviors. If children do well early, and are positively evaluated by their teachers, parents are likely to respond more positively towards education. The college students' parents' positive valuation of education was **reinforced** by their children's early positive school experiences. The nonstudents' parents, who often saw that their children were not "doing well" early, were more likely to see their less enthusiastic attitudes toward education reinforced as well.

Parental values, then, are more dynamic than static. The values of the respondents' parents were affected by their work experiences, which did change over time. As people occupy different occupational positions, due to upward mobility and changing market conditions, their perspective also changes. As their children experience early success or failure in school, parents' attitudes concerning education may evolve. Thus, nuclear family dynamics and processes are not immune to societal influences.

Coleman and Rainwater (1978) developed a multidimensional conception of social class that accounts for differences within each of three major classes: upper, middle, and working. Their view is that "behavioral and value variables" help account for status differences both between and within each major class. In my Life Stories research, I found significant differences within the working class. Noticeable differences in work experiences, values, and behaviors between the families of most of the college students, on the one hand, and the nonstudents, on the other, are consistent with Coleman and Rainwater's discussion.

FRIENDS' INFLUENCES

Friends also are important in the socialization of children, and children's peer associations may influence their educational aspirations. Alexander and Campbell (1964), studying parents with the same education levels, found that, if a child's best friend planned to attend college, then that child was more likely to attend college. Carpenter and Fleishman (1987) found that having friends who planned to attend college encouraged high school seniors to plan to attend college. Why and how a child chooses such friends may be important. I investigated friendship patterns and choices within the working class in the Life Stories research, and my findings were very similar.

A recent study (Nebbitt, Lombe, LaPoint, and Bryant 2009) found that children's attitudes about deviance and exposure to delinquent peers affected school performance. Children who had "unfavorable attitudes towards deviance" were more likely to do well in school. Children who were more likely to become involved in antisocial behavior and had more contacts with "delinquent peers" were less likely to do well in school. (Nebbitt, Lombe, LaPoint, and Bryant 2009.)

SCHOOL EXPERIENCES

Persell (1977) suggests that the key purpose of the public schools is to separate students from one another, into "good" and "bad" students. This separation often is based on test scores, and, since the tests themselves are set up with middle class standards in mind, there are subtle social class biases in the evaluation process. Oakes (1985), Bowles and Gintis (1976), and Jencks et al. (1972) all suggest that social class, values, and tracking all affect one another.

Hotchkiss and Dorsten (1987) found that high school students who were in a "high prestige academic curriculum" were more likely to attend college than high school students who were not. Time enrolled in college, a measure of eventual success in the completion of a degree, also was affected in the same direction by the positive tracking. According to Alexander, Cook, and McDill (1978):

> tracking consistently affects educational goals, achievements, and goal-oriented behaviors in the twelfth grade, and is often the most important factor of those included in our model. Being in a college track increases the probability of applying to college and enhances one's prospects for being admitted. In these ways, sorting processes within high school may substantially affect later socioeconomic attainments.

Alexander, Cook, and McDill noted the importance of social class background factors in influencing the type of program in which secondary school students are enrolled. They also found that, when looking at students in the same social class, positive tracking still has positive effects on long-term educational attainment. Similarly, negative tracking has negative long-term effects on educational attainment, regardless of class background.

In another study, curriculum tracking was the key component of the inheritance of a manual class position, of the variables tested (Colclough and Beck 1986). Students from "manual class backgrounds" were much more likely to be tracked negatively into a vocational track, and students from "mental class" backgrounds were much more likely to be in a college bound track.

These findings strongly suggest that the high school experiences of working class children should be considered, in order to more fully understand the tracking process. Specifically, significant differences in school experiences within the working class may help explain why some working class children eventually attend college, and others do not. These very differences in school experiences were explored in depth and detail in my Life Stories research. From that research, I conclude that there is no doubt that school experiences through high school definitely influence whether or not working class children attend college. As so many other studies have concluded, those earlier school experiences are extremely important.

BECOMING A COLLEGE ATTENDER: THE SOCIALIZATION PROCESS

The process of producing a working class college attender typically begins in childhood. The college attenders in my Life Stories research developed strong work habits concerning completing their homework in their early school years. Many became "self motivated," and this served them well, as they surpassed the educational levels their parents had achieved. Doing their homework also helped them become successful students early in their school days, and this early success set the stage for future academic success.

The family clearly was the single most important agent of socialization, for both the college student and nonstudent respondents, in the Life Stories research. Although cousins, aunts, and uncles occasionally were important in influencing the educational aspirations of the respondents, members of the nuclear family clearly were most significant. The fact that in the large majority of the student respondents' nuclear families all of the college age siblings attended college further supports this conclusion. Non-nuclear relatives who influenced the respondents were much more likely to augment the nuclear family influences in the same direction rather than the reverse. Very few respondents were exceptions to any of these generalizations.

Within the nuclear family, the mother of the student respondent typically was the single most influential person pertaining to educational aspirations. Mothers spent more time with the students than their fathers did, and the time spent together often was quality time. Student respondents, both female and male, most often singled out their mothers as the loved one who "kept tabs" on them concerning schoolwork.

Open communication also was most evident between the student respondents and their mothers. It was their mothers in whom student respondents most often confided, and with whom they discussed their problems and anxieties. In fact, for many of the student respondents, their mothers were extremely important people in their lives. Many described their relationships with their mothers in very positive terms, and very enthusiastically. It was not uncommon for a student respondent to describe her or his mother as "my best friend."

That the mothers usually were the principal care givers of the children in these families certainly facilitated developing these strong relationships with their children. This necessary condition, however, was not a sufficient one. The mothers of the college students seemed to possess special qualities as parents, confidants, and mentors of a sort. The college students' mothers understood the importance of a college education, although they typically lacked such an education. Yet, they were very effective in transmitting that valuation of education to their children, with the skills of master teachers.

The critical importance of open communication is further noted by variation within the student respondent category. Open communication clearly was common among the student respondents' families in general. Among those student respondents who were the first in their respective families to attend college (the "pioneers"), open communication was nearly **universal**. It is through open communication that the students' parents transmitted their high valuation of education to their children. This was most important among the pioneers. Since no one in their families could serve as true "modelers," open communication with parents strengthened their parents' influence as "definers" (Cohen 1987).

The importance of these characteristics is further emphasized by their absence among the nonstudent respondents. Typically, no one kept tabs on the nonstudent respondents concerning education to any significant degree. Open communication rarely existed between the nonstudents and their parents. Few of the nonstudents' parents valued education or emphasized education to the nonstudent respondents in any significant way.

Open communication between the college students and their parents also likely had other positive effects for the students. Open communication encourages children to ask questions and seek answers. In the home, parents likely are the authority figures towards whom children direct their questions. Such children seem likely to ask questions of other authority figures as well. In school, they logically would ask more questions of teachers, and pursue answers in an academic setting. This might encourage reading, attentiveness in class, and independent pursuit of knowledge. These skills and inclinations likely correlate with both positive assessment from teachers and academic success. This all is a classic example of what I call "motion in the same direction."

In addition to encouraging their children to ask questions, open communication and frequent conversations between the college student respondents and their parents likely accelerated the students' language development. Logically, this contributed to the early academic success of the college student respondents. Most college students' early childhood experiences of open communication, frequent conversations, and early academic success stand in stark contrast with the experiences of the nonstudent respondents: little open communication and much less successful school experiences.

The educational attainments of the small number of longest college attenders among the nonstudent respondents also fit. Concerning the key factors that correlate with college attendance, these respondents are situated in the gray area between the typical college student respondent, on the one hand, and the typical nonstudent respondent who never attended college, on the other. This suggests that the presence of some, but not all, of the significant factors increases the likelihood of some educational aspirations and attainments beyond high school. Typically, however, this does not result in the completion of at least a four year college degree.

The college bound working class respondents usually associated with peers most of whom also were college bound. The college students developed friendships with classmates in the schools they attended. These friends often became more important than their neighborhood friends. Friendships developed with people of similar orientation and often replaced childhood friendships more typically based on proximity.

The nonstudent respondents usually had friends growing up who like themselves were not college bound. Their school friends and neighborhood friends were similar to one another, and they typically shared a disinterest in academics. The nonstudent respondents were more likely to be popular and less likely to be ostracized by their peers than were the college student respondents.

Like the non-nuclear relatives, the friends of the respondents typically augmented the influences of their parents concerning educational aspirations in the same direction. Some nonstudents had parents who did not value education, but some friends who did. In these cases, the friends were not able to influence the nonstudents to aspire to attend college. This supports the conclusion that parents were the most important agents of socialization.

RECENT TRENDS AND FUTURE PROJECTIONS

If decreasing upward mobility and increasing downward mobility (Newman 1993; 1988) should continue, then the implications for working class children are not good. Without a doubt, life for millions of working class families has become much more difficult in the early 2000's, and especially during the worst recession since The Great Depression. If fewer working class parents can move up into the upper reaches of the working class, then fewer working class families will be positioned to launch their children into college. Cuts in federal college financial aid programs and rising costs of higher education together likely will make launching new pioneers more difficult.

Another set of factors also may reduce the number of college attenders from the working class. The income share of the lowest 60% of American families has declined since 1981 (Bureau of the Census 2010). If this trend should continue, then fewer working class families will be able to afford to live in "better" neighborhoods. This would further entrench class based housing segregation. Working class children therefore would be less likely to have middle class families as neighbors, and more likely to attend high schools with few middle class students. The result likely will be separate and unequal schools.

Working class families' general financial deterioration would negatively impact the educational aspirations of working class children. Parents likely will find it more difficult to "help" their children with college expenses and tuition. The children likely would be compelled to work more hours per week, take fewer credits per semester, or both. Given the hectic schedules and very heavy work loads of most of the college student respondents in the Life Stories research, that scenario is not encouraging.

These broader societal realities squeeze the working class from opposite directions. As college costs continue to rise, working class children will find it harder to attend college. As the number of more stable, better paying working class jobs continues to dwindle, working class people can expect to find earning a decent living without a college education increasingly more difficult. The gap between the haves and have nots will continue to grow from a creek to a canyon. These realities may inspire Americans to reevaluate their conception of the American class system as open and fluid (Coleman and Rainwater 1978).

Overall, unless federal policies and the relative economic standing of working class families change significantly, the struggle to attend college will intensify for aspiring college attenders of working class origins. Given worsening economic conditions, the long term employment prospects for working class people who lack a college education will be dismal. By becoming more aware of these realities, working class people may better equip themselves and their children to effect change, at both the family level and in American society. Ultimately, what appears to be a "trouble" (due to individuals' actions or "failings") in actuality is an "issue" (Mills 1959), the resolution of which must occur at the societal level.

Working class parents can and must be strong, positive messengers to their children in these hard times. Imparting the entire message is critically important, and parents should not pull any punches. First, teach your children that working class families have suffered greatly during the first decade of the twenty first century, then tell them why. Working people have lost jobs and income primarily **because** they are **not** college educated. The waves of foreclosures that have resulted also were fueled by rampant overconsumption and the spending of money that people did not have to spend without the availability of "generous" credit terms. Secondly, the time tested way for your children (and most people) to significantly increase their income and decrease their risk of future layoffs **is** to get a four year college degree. Then, your children would be in a position to actually afford the opulent lifestyle. Of course, if they are as wise as their parents, they will choose not to overindulge themselves, except perhaps for the added *extravagance* of a professional degree.

PART FOUR

HOW YOU COULD HELP YOUR CHILD OR GRANDCHILD

11

WHAT PARENTS AND GRANDPARENTS COULD DO

Any parent or grandparent will tell you that parents typically have profound effects on their children. Much of this book has discussed parental influences, both the obvious and the subtle. At this point in our discussion, we should summarize what quite a bit of social science research has to say about how parents influence their children's educational aspirations. What type of family environment helps parents get their pro education messages across to their children? What helps build academic and life skills? What encourages children to do well in school? How does money come into play? How can a less than ideal financial situation be used as a "teaching tool?" What can parents and grandparents do, to set a good example? In sum, how can you, as a concerned parent or grandparent, influence your young loved ones to aspire to attend college? Upon further review, the answers will become obvious.

OPEN COMMUNICATION AND STRUCTURE

"Open Communication" simply means that the lines of communication always remain open between parents and their child. Ideally, a child always should be able to talk to her parents about almost anything, although this ideal is rarely achieved. In practical terms, open communication means that a child always will feel comfortable thinking about talking to his parents about a problem or issue, and this will make it much more likely that the child will actually do so. This, in turn, will increase the likelihood that a child will speak to parents and/or other authority figures (like teachers) before making a decision that will seriously impact his life or his future. One component of fostering open communication with your child is for you to try to become comfortable talking about subjects that you really are uncomfortable talking about. Sex is one such topic for many American parents. If you hope that your child eventually will attend college, she or he should avoid having any part in an unplanned pregnancy at a young age. Numerous studies prove that children having children often results in both the boy and the girl not graduating from high school. Colleges today require applicants to have successfully completed high school, or "the equivalent," before they can be admitted. One cannot graduate from college if one cannot even "get in." Long term poverty, especially for the girl and the baby, is another common consequence of two teenagers having a baby out of wedlock.

A teenage girl thinking about "sleeping with her boyfriend" might speak to her parents or her older sister before doing so, if open communication is rule number one in her family's household. If she does speak to her mom or dad in advance of the activity, she will be less likely to be pushed into a dangerous or potentially life-altering situation. Her boyfriend's hasty, hormone driven "sweet talking" will be tempered by the wisdom of an adult's perspective on having sex. Such lucky children are much more likely to avoid both sexually transmitted diseases and unplanned pregnancies. Unplanned teenage pregnancies inevitably bring significant negative and life-altering consequences into children's lives.

Open communication between parents and their child is critically important for the child, for many other reasons. What if your child is thinking about drinking, or getting into other drugs besides alcohol? What if her friends are drinking, and she does not want to, but her friends (and her horny boyfriend) are pushing her to do so? If she can come to you, she will, and she might avoid both teenage pregnancy, and driving in a car with a drunk at the wheel. My guess is that most of today's parents in the United States have had some experience with sex, drinking, other drugs, and/or driving. Why not create an opportunity to share the wisdom of your years by fostering an environment in which your child willingly and actively seeks the counsel of your wisdom?

What if your child has a problem with homework, or with a student harassing her, or with a teacher disrespecting him? Only in an open communication forum will your child let you know what is going on. Then, you could either offer suggestions, or intervene, as you see fit. If your child is being bullied, for example, you might offer a number of good, useful, informed, intellectual suggestions if he comes to you. "Study the martial arts" is one piece of advice I have heard. "Get a big crow bar" is another. (Just kidding!) Would you rather be in a position to help defuse the situation, or read about it in shock some day, with your child on page one of every newspaper from coast to coast? As a parent, the choice is yours, and then, your child's.

Open communication does not mean that parents and their child all are equal partners in their relationship. Too many parents buy into the "Let the Child Explore" mindset in American society today, and children (and society) are suffering because of it. I personally learned this lesson the hard way, when my "nephew" was five or six. My wife Linda and I volunteered to take my friend's son to The Bronx Zoo for the day. Linda, who had a Bachelor's degree in Childhood Education at the time, was clearly the more informed of the two "adults" present. When we got to the zoo, I said to the kid: "You can go see whatever you want." Three seconds later, I was frantically chasing a speeding kid who was exploring the entire Bronx Zoo, and Linda was laughing, and shaking her head in utter disbelief. Set limits for kids. The adult should be in charge. Structure is important for children. Despite all these 'restrictions," you still can have fun together. We did. Lessons learned, the hard way, as usual.

Some parents "negotiate" with their children, which often means that kids get their way, even if it is not in their best long term interests. I have seen countless examples of this, and I am sure that you have, too. Revisiting my homework war from first grade, if my mom had been a negotiator, it would have gone like this: "Oh, Michael, would you please do your homework now? If you do, maybe I can talk to dad about working a third job, so we won't have to break open your piggy bank to buy linoleum for our bedroom before your dad trips and breaks his neck. If he did break his neck, then he might be a little disappointed, and he couldn't even work two jobs to keep a roof over our heads. Now, you wouldn't want your dad to break his neck, would you?" *Pull eaze!*

As a parent, you are not your child's friend, even though, in openly communicative family relationships, a child often says that "my mom is my best friend." That was the case for many of the college students in my Life Stories research. As long as your child thinks that you are her best friend, she will talk to you about anything important. That means that she will not make an important decision without first soliciting your informed adult parental opinion. That is not child abuse; that is authoritative and good parenting. It works very well, for both parent and child, especially in the long run.

To me, one key to "Authoritative Parenting" (Dornbusch, et al. 1987) is to **be** the parent, not the child's friend. A second key is open communication. A third key is to have rules, stick to the rules (without being inflexible and rigid), and explain to your child why the rules are rules as often as possible. A system of rewards and punishments also is very important. Physical, emotional and/or psychological abuses of children definitely are not part of authoritative parenting.

If you want to be involved in your child's life, involve your child in your life. Take your child to work with you, to a ball game, to a museum, to the library. Make the time, or find the time, to do things with your child. Do things with your child that matter to him, not to you. Don't try to convince him to love football; instead, find out what he likes, and try to convince yourself to love or at least tolerate that. Be fair, and treat your child as an equal, although it might best remain our little secret that you are not equal. You, as the parent, must have 51% of the votes in all significant "elections" or decisions that you and your child make together. You also should provide a "united front" together with the child's other parent, if at all possible. As I tell my students, the first thing that a child learns to do is "divide and conquer," pitting one parent against the other. It goes something like this: "Well, mommy said I could do this," or "daddy said I can do that." If a child asks you if she can do something, tell her: "I will talk to your mother (or father), and then we will let you know what our decision is." This approach avoids letting the child get the first and possibly last word in with your partner. If you give him the opening, he will run to mom, and plead with her, until he has won her vote. Then, you and she will be arguing about it, often in front of the child. Then, the child already has won. Negotiators put themselves in such situations; real parents don't. If you have a child, you must be a parent to that child; it is basic biology and common sense, nothing more.

DOING WELL IN SCHOOL

Numerous studies, including my Doctoral Dissertation research, have proven that children who do well in school early have a tendency to continue to do well in school, as they grow older. Doing well in school begins with effort, that is, hard work, early and often. Teach your children the work ethic that you yourself have. No matter how intelligent or disadvantaged any child is, she or he can only improve with additional effort. To help instill a work ethic in your child, require the child to contribute at home by doing chores (within reason). Examples include helping with the grocery shopping, putting away the groceries, cleaning, laundry, helping with dinner preparation, putting out the garbage, yard work or anything else that seems fair and appropriate, given the child's age, talents and abilities. (There is no free lunch.) If you as a working parent are pressed for time, by including your child in the dinner preparation and cleanup, for example, you share activities that are necessary. You also create more free time for you to share with your child. There is nothing wrong with that, despite numerous societal pressures to overindulge or spoil your child instead. Since everyone eats, everyone should help clean up, too. The work ethic, once instilled, becomes an asset that serves the child well throughout her lifetime. It is astonishing to me how many American children today appear to lack a strong work ethic. I can only suggest that, if your child does have a strong work ethic, he will have much less competition than many of us realize.

I remember what my boss Pete at the trucking company (where I worked full time for 14 years) said to me one day. I was waiting for a helper to come in, and Pete was telling me that the guy "was good." He then said: "I knew what kind of worker you were, the first time I saw you walk in here." I questioned him. "How? What do you mean?" I asked. He replied: "You came in a half hour early, you had a bounce in your step, and you looked like you were ready to do a day's work." Who would you hire? Believe me, you are not doing your child any favors handing him everything that he has, for free, on a silver platter. All you are teaching him that way is to expect a free lunch. If, on the other hand, your child has to work for privileges and luxuries, she will learn that luxuries are hard to come by, and work is not optional, but required. Those are valuable lifelong lessons that she will apply to many aspects of her life and future.

Speaking of luxuries, I very strongly recommend that you and your child read *Rich Dad, Poor Dad*, written by Robert Kiyosaki and Sharon Lechter. I think it is a great book, written by two college graduates who know a thing or two about finances, and have a lot of common sense. I find most so called luxuries to be distractions, and rarely worth what they cost. (For example, I would rather have fifty $10. bottles of wine than one $500. bottle of wine. Is that one bottle of very expensive wine really fifty times as tasty as one of those cheaper bottles of wine? Fifty bottles of wine would last much longer, unless you have a lot of thirsty friends.) I also have learned that if you are spending money that you do not have on luxuries that you cannot afford, that is not the way to "financial security." If you value luxuries, and do not value education, you might have a little trouble ever getting any luxuries. You also may recall that the college students from my Life Stories research were much more concerned about relationships than material things growing up. The nonstudents, on the other hand, were more concerned with material things than relationships. The working class families that emphasized relationships (the "relational" families) tended to send their children to college. The working class families that emphasized material possessions typically did not send their children to college.

What does a strong work ethic have to do with doing well in school early on? For one thing, doing homework obviously requires effort and time. By doing homework well early in the process, the student is conditioning the teacher to expect both effort and a good result from that student. That most certainly encourages the teacher to have a more positive attitude about that student in the future. The student feels good about herself and likes school. That encourages both good attendance and continued efforts to do well. Research often strongly suggests that teacher's expectations do affect students' performance (Persell, 1977).

A strong work ethic also encourages a young student to become self motivated. Self motivation relates to doing homework well, in part because the self motivated student is not wasting energy fighting with a parent about doing homework. Effort therefore is applied to what **really** matters: doing homework well and early. As a child's high energy level eventually wanes as the day progresses, doing homework well becomes more of a challenge. In addition, the self motivated student eventually will be better able to complete assignments in the later grades on her own. Parents, although willing, might not have the expertise and education to help at that point. Of course, most parents do occasionally help their children with homework, and, in a family with open communication, children are likely to turn to parents for such help. Turning to the teacher for help also is a good idea, especially in the later grades. If the student already has a positive relationship with the teacher, help will be more freely offered by the teacher and accepted by the student. As a parent, you can insure that your child has a positive relationship with the teacher by developing a relationship with the teacher yourself. Obviously, there should be boundaries (!), but you need to know what is going on in school. You also need to know how your child is doing in school, and the teacher needs your support and reassurance. You also must reinforce what the teacher is doing in the classroom at home as much as you can. This means finding the time for parent/teacher conferences, speaking to the teacher regularly, and developing and fostering open communication between you and the teacher. You also must keep tabs on the teacher, to insure that the teacher also is applying effort and is concerned. Assume that the teacher is working hard, and is dedicated, unless proven otherwise. Many teachers, in my opinion, are caring, qualified, and dedicated professionals. Too many parents today look to blame teachers for most or all of their child's failings. I would look first to the **effort** that your child is applying. Be honest and as objective as possible in your assessments. You must advocate for your child, but this does **not** mean that the child should be running the classroom! As is the case at home, the adult should be in charge. By being actively involved with your child's education, you significantly increase the likelihood that your child will do well in school (Henderson, 1987; Orthner, Jones-Sanpei, Hair, and Moore, et al., 2009; Murray, 2009; Lopez Turley, Desmond, and Bruch, 2010). Parents who have open and positive relationships with their children's teachers often see positive results in the children's academic work (Henderson, 1987).

What if your child has learning disabilities or other circumstances that make learning more challenging? The same basic rules apply, with some notable exceptions. First, the real problem is "the system." I have stated in some of my classes that "the system itself is learning disabled," and that "the system tends to sort and separate people based on everything but ability." The system often tries to force everyone to learn the same way and to follow the rules almost blindly. I have no illusions. I know now for a fact that I myself am learning disabled. My learning disabilities never were detected or even suspected in school, and yet, I have a Ph.D. How did that happen? Through a lot of hard work, and a little luck, I was able to navigate through the system successfully. After twenty five plus years of teaching college, I am flabbergasted at how many professors (and therefore, I assume, classroom teachers in general) are completely clueless about learning disabilities and other impediments to many students realizing their potential. So, if you are the parent of a special child, you absolutely must educate yourself, advocate for your child, and then educate any clueless educators who come anywhere near your child. Advocate, and educate, but remember that, on a certain level at least, "Annie Sullivan was right!" Until Helen Keller's most effective teacher was able to gain some level of control, as the adult, over her blind and deaf pupil, she had little chance of teaching her very much. Helen eventually learned that, instead of being handed everything, she would have to work very hard to begin to compensate for her loss of sight and hearing. Learning disabilities and physical challenges are all too real. For any truly challenged child to have a chance in this system, that child must work twice as hard. That extra effort, in conjunction with good teachers, determined parents, devices, and techniques, will maximize the possibilities. Effort is the one factor over which your child has some real control. Teach your child to apply maximum effort to increase the possibilities of successes.

Lack of structure and discipline, in combination with an all too real, serious, and debilitating condition, can have significant negative consequences. I witnessed an example of this one fine day in the grocery store. As I was browsing by the vegetables, a boy, perhaps seven or eight, ran into the store alone. He immediately began to pull numerous items off countless shelves, weaving a path of destruction like a speeding, two legged tornado. I watched and waited, fully expecting to eventually see the parent, sauntering leisurely behind. When I finally saw the adult, who walked into the store slowly, I called out to him and pointed to the boy as he ran around the corner: "Is that your child?" He looked at me. I continued: "He's pulling stuff off all the shelves!" He replied: "He has X (a very real disorder/disability). Do you know what that *means*?" I answered: "I have a Ph.D., and I'm a college professor, and my wife has been teaching children (with that disorder/disability) for twelve years. (This was all true at the time.) I know what X means. Does it mean that he can do whatever the hell he wants to do, and destroy the store?" Before he could respond, I continued: "You're going to pick up all that stuff, aren't you? You're going to pick up all that stuff!" I probably looked a little scary at that point. I can't help it; it comes naturally. I waited for him to comply. He did. Driving home from the store, I thought: That kid really has two problems. He has a very real disorder/disability, **and** he's a spoiled brat! From my wife Linda's experiences, I am fully aware how difficult it is to teach children with disorders and disabilities. Although there is some ongoing and promising research, there are as of yet few definitive answers. I doubt that "let the kid do whatever he wants" is one real solution.

One final word on encouraging your child to do well in school: NO TV! If they must watch TV, homework first, please! Have you ever really watched a two year old watch TV? (That can be a little scary, don't you think?) With a few exceptions, I doubt that watching a lot of TV is much good for anyone, especially younger children. Many television shows distort reality. So, if you want to punish your child, force him to watch a lot of TV! That might work. Seriously, one of today's popular "punishments" for misbehaving children is to "send them to their rooms." I doubt that most of the kids whose rooms are fully equipped, with TV, stereo, DVD player, computer, IPOD, phone, countless toys and games, and all the latest technology actually feel like they are *being* punished. To me, real punishment for misdeeds would be to take away some or all of those privileges that their parents' hard earned money likely paid for.

What might you and your child do, instead of watching TV? If your child is young, you might have a conversation, or read to the child. Then, as the child gets a little older, you might read with the child. Finally, the child might read to you or to herself. You also each might read the same book, and then, discuss it! (This book might be one option.) You as a parent can set an example yourself by reading. Your child will emulate and imitate you, as every parent knows. Why not encourage your child to develop a lifelong habit that will increase the likelihood for academic success? Reading at a young age facilitates early language development, and helps children do well in school early. This increases the chance that the child will continue to do well in school later, because old habits are hard to break.

Looking for a gift idea for a birthday or holiday? Give a child, any child in your circle, books, encyclopedias, a computer, internet access, software that facilitates real learning, anything but a TV and more toys. Most American children have too many toys anyway. Imagine two children, one of whom has dozens of baseballs and bats, and the other has one of each. What is each child really learning from his respective circumstances? The child with many bats and balls probably takes a bat and a ball for granted. Losing one ball is a big deal to the child with only one ball. He likely takes good care of his lone baseball, while the other child has them strewn all over his yard. Offer them something that will help stimulate their minds to develop fully. Remember, use it or lose it. Have you ever watched a two year old watch TV?

TEACH CHILDREN ABOUT MONEY, AND HOW HARD IT IS TO MAKE

There are one million books out there, it seems, that teach people how to be financial wizards and get rich quick. These books focus on real estate, stocks, business ventures, and other investments that in reality all require some start up investment capital, in order to truly have long term growth potential. For most people, start up capital comes from surplus income. How do you earn surplus income? Earn more than you spend, and save the rest. How do you earn significantly more money in your own lifetime? Complete a four year college degree. These are the most important facts about money that any parent can teach any child, regardless of income or education level. Talk is cheap, you say. What can I really teach my kid about money, you might ask, since I always have so little of it? You might lament, for example, that "I wish I had gone to college. Then, I probably would be my boss' *boss* by now!" Intentionally or not, you do set an example for your child with **everything** that you say and do. By being frugal (not cheap!), you teach your child that money is hard to come by, and not to be thrown away. By spending money on what really matters (like books and other educational materials), you teach your child about real, dependable long term investments on a limited income. By discussing your own work experiences with your child, you give your child a sense of how hard you work, and how frustrating any job can be at times. By discussing the demands and limits of your own job, whether they are financial, physical, psychological, or whatever, you encourage your child to look elsewhere, and "higher." Since talk really is cheap, the most effective "teaching tool" is experience. Take your child to work with you!

If you are a secretary, let your daughter or son witness how disrespectful some bosses can be to their subordinates, even though that secretary actually may be running the office! If your job is physically very demanding, let your son or daughter actually **do** some hard labor. If your job can be dull or repetitive, let your child be bored to tears. If you can manipulate your work setting, let your child work his or her butt off, and go home dog tired, frustrated, or angry. Most jobs, from my experience, offer workers that particular opportunity. Play it up! Give your child a glimpse of the very worst that your job can offer, and a full day or week or summer of it, if you can arrange it. As a concerned parent, it is your duty to give your child such a bad taste of the work world without a college degree that the child will run to college like it was an all you can eat twenty four hour ice cream parlor! If you do it right, you will leave a lasting impression. I had many of those, not only from working with my dad, but from my own work experiences driving a truck. One day in particular carved a deep canyon in my memory banks. I was working with one of my older partners, a man who was in his fifties at the time. We had a Brooklyn home delivery run, with quite a few multiple flight walkups. After lugging a heavy washing machine up three or four flights of stairs, my partner was extremely winded, and gasping for air. I thought he was going to have a heart attack. (I had seen that level of exhaustion on that job many times.) I was barely breathing hard, since I was very strong and a very well conditioned serious athlete in my early twenties at the time. I took one long hard look at him, saw my own future, and screamed to myself under my breath: "I've got to get the hell out of here!" I mumbled that particular mantra countless additional times on the trucking job after that fateful day. Going to college definitely looked much more attractive and promising to me from that day forward.

TEACH YOUR CHILD WHY

At this point, you have read most of this book, and yet, you are still reading. You must be a glutton for punishment! What have you learned from the utterances on these pages? As I say all the time, if you understand the why, you can deal with any how. Try to make it painfully clear to your child any way that you can why she or he must attend college. You certainly don't need this book, although I hope that it helps you a bit in your honorable quest. You are a worker in a society that often punishes people who do not have college degrees. You can teach your own children from your own work experiences what they are likely to face if they do not attend college. As you well know, they are likely to face a lifetime of struggle, frustration and listening to educated idiots telling them what to do and how to do it. You already know that; simply pass it on to them.

WHY NOT SET A REALLY GOOD EXAMPLE?

Up until now, I have been pulling my best punches, so as not to hurt your feelings or your solar plexus. Why not attend college yourself?

I know, you are too old to do that at this point in your life. Give me a break. I finally finished my Ph.D. at age 43, so I know what you are thinking. My wife Linda recently completed her second Master's degree at age 55. In graduate school, I thought about quitting **every** day. I also have taught many "returning adults" as a college professor for many years, so I've heard this particular copout many times before. How could I go to college? We can't afford it. I have no time. I'm not smart enough. (One semester as a college student will teach you that there probably are many idiots with Ph.D.'s, and some of them are professors!) Many of my returning adult college students have told me that they thought of quitting, but my "speeches" or my "stories" kept them from doing so. (Remember, I am not a fiction writer; I write from experience.) Most of my mature adult students, in fact, eventually did get their four year degrees. Many, in fact, went on to earn Master's degrees as well. Yeah, I know, blah blah blah from another talking head. Did you forget that I drove a freakin' delivery truck full time for fourteen years? I also worked full time while earning my Bachelor's, two Master's, and a Doctorate. I know you can retire in two or three years. So what? What are you going to do then? If you earned your Bachelor's degree, and then retired, you could collect your pension, and then go out and earn more money working fewer hours. Some employers, in fact, help pay for their employees' educations, so you might be better off earning your degree while you are working. Why not set a real example for your kids by taking a college class or two yourself?

Perhaps you really are too old. One of my older students said that about herself during class one night. We were chatting during the break, and she said: "What am I doing here? I'm an old lady!" I asked her how old she was. She told me that she was in her early fifties. She actually was older than me at the time, and I was her professor! I asked her: "In four years, how much older will you be?" She responded: "Four years older." I replied: "So, in four years, you are going to be four years older anyway. You may as well have four more years of education!" She stayed in school, earned her Bachelor's degree, and a Master's degree in social work. She became a practicing social worker, and a very good one, I have no doubt. After all, this woman worked many years in the real world, raised a special child, and learned how to become an effective advocate, by fighting for her own child. Wouldn't she make a great social worker? Only if she earned her college degrees. Why not earn yours?

I know, it would be too hard. Most of my returning adult students work full time, help support families, care for children, and attend classes nights and/or weekends. Few are independently wealthy, primarily because they do not have college degrees! They certainly struggle, but most of them have come to the realization that they will struggle more in the future, unless they earn their college degrees. So, they juggle work, family, and school, but school most definitely stays on their "to do" lists. They chip away, and before they realize it, they earn their Bachelor's degrees. Then, they often come back for more, so they are gluttons for punishment too. The difference is that they are inflicting punishment on themselves for very good reasons: long term financial security, and a better, more fulfilling work experience in the future. They are working very hard for a few years to earn a four year degree, so that they will not have to continue to work very hard to get nowhere for the rest of their lives!

Finally, you surrender, and you're convinced. 'Where do I start?' you ask. Start by taking an introductory course in something that you think sounds interesting at your local community college, one night per week. Register for a crowded class; it is probably crowded for a good reason. Check it out. Get your feet wet. Taste one flavor. Just do it! Get in one class. Chat with your fellow students. You will find that many are in the same leaky boat that you're in, and that a few are a bit ahead of you in the process. Talk to the professor, if she or he actually is a human being, rather than a talking head or a suit. It's your life. You have the power to make it better, in the long term, if you choose to try. Working extra hours, at your present job, or working part time, at a second job, is not going to get you there, unless you have a degree or two. I earn more at my part time job than many Americans earn at their full time jobs, because I have a couple of degrees. You could do the same, in time, like many of my former students now do!

How do you pay for it? How do you think I paid for it, with my trust fund? I had nearly fifty thousand dollars in school loans when I finally graduated in 1995. Fortunately, I found a full time teaching position the same week that I defended my doctoral dissertation, so that helped. It took me ten years to pay off those loans. During that time, I drove a car (a 1977 Chevy Impala station wagon) that my dad had given to me after my engine went on another car when I was a little poor. The car had 120,000 miles on it when I took possession. When I finally junked that car, it had 455,000 miles on it! My students often made fun of my car, and laughed about it. One day during a class, when a large group of students who knew me well were really raggin' on my car, I said: "I put over 300,000 miles on a car that I got for free. How many new cars would that be?" The class agreed that two new cars would be the rough equivalent. I continued: "So, you paid off two new car loans; I paid off my Ph.D. from Columbia University. Who got ahead?" I still had the car, and I still have the Ph.D. You found the money for that giant screen TV, status symbol car, and/or the six cell phones your family owns. Frankly, you could blow enough money to pay for one college course at a community college in a few hours, if you take your family and yourself to a ballgame! A long family weekend trip to a big "theme park" (including air fare, rental car, hotels, food and souvenirs) probably would cost more today than an Associate's degree from your local community college! Stop making excuses! Invest a little money in something that really matters: education. Do it for yourself! Remember, you probably are reading this book because you hope that your child or grandchild eventually will attend college. So, forget about yourself. Do it for them. Set a good example by attending college yourself, and if you stay long enough, you will earn your degree. That will put you in a better position to help them pay for their degrees, because you will earn more money. When you really break it down, it's a no brainer, isn't it? So, why not go to college *yourself*?

KEYS TO COLLEGE

1. Value education, and teach its importance
2. Keep tabs on school and homework
3. Read, and encourage reading
4. Open communication
5. Honesty about "family economics"
6. There is no free lunch. Give your children the work ethic, not "a lot of stuff"
7. Authoritative parenting
8. Push children to have "a better life" than you have: by going to college
9. Encourage your children to explore and develop all their talents and interests
10. Be the best example: take a college course yourself!

12

A NOTE TO THE STUDENT

Tens of millions of Americans have attended college. You are about to join their ranks. Many of those students who eventually earned their four year college degrees had anxiety as their first semester approached. Most professional athletes are nervous before an important game. Most "superstar" singers feel butterflies before each performance. The President of the United States is uneasy before giving the State of the Union Address. Why would you be any less human than they are? You are taking the first steps in the next phase of your life. The journey ahead inevitably will lead you to a much more rewarding and satisfying future, so embrace the opportunity.

COLLEGE IS THE NEXT STEP

After you have graduated from high school, college simply is the next logical step. It is a step that you clearly were not ready to take after ninth grade, but now that you have finished twelfth grade, you are ready. I am shocked by how many of my returning adult college students think that they are not ready for college. Many of the college students in my Life Stories research said: "I wasn't ready for college when I got there." In some significant ways, college is different from high school, but it is only the next step up, after high school. There is a period of adjustment to the new routines, the new surroundings, and the new people. Your freshman year is that period of transition and adjustment. Every college graduate has gone through this unsettling time; you soon will join that group. All you have to do to graduate is stay in college long enough, and do some work! Ultimately, college is primarily an endurance test.

Making friends during your freshman year clearly will help you adjust to college. Remind yourself that everyone in your first year classes is either in the same boat that you are in, or recently was in that boat. So, talk to your fellow students! Chat with classmates before class, in the hallways, and wherever you see a familiar face, but not during class! Joining an athletic team, club, or other campus activity or organization is one sure way to make new friends, and adjust more easily to the new routines. You will be most uncomfortable during your first week, but both the first week and your discomfort will pass very quickly. Simply ride the wave, because it is the beginning of a very important journey.

There is one significant difference between high school and college that you should become aware of as soon as possible. Although each college course typically will require you to do more work than you might be used to doing, there is much less oversight of that work. What I mean is that you will be given course requirements, reading lists, and the like, but there will not be someone standing over you every day, to make certain that "you read Chapter 5 by next Tuesday." As I like to tell my students, it all comes out in the wash. If you do not do your work, you will suffer the consequences, and "no one will care." Remind yourself that you probably got this far because you have a strong work ethic, and not because you inherited a trust fund. So, simply do what good students do: do your work! You probably will need to pick up the pace a bit, but you will adjust well in time. Expect your first year to be your year of adjustments, and, as you adjust, your work and therefore your grades will improve. Most college grads with good cums (cumulative grade point averages) do their best work as they approach their graduations.

DEALING WITH PROFESSORS

I myself was a college student for nearly twenty years, earning a Bachelor's degree, two Master's degrees, and a Ph.D. degree while working full time. As an adjunct (part time) professor working at several different colleges at the same time, I pieced together "full time" work and eeked out a living as I was completing my doctoral dissertation. I have been a "real" full time professor for sixteen years. I have taught at a total of seventeen different campuses of eight different colleges and universities for more than a quarter century. That is a lot of experience with the college routine, from both sides of the fence. I often have been accused of being "too honest" with students by both administrators and colleagues. Where I came from, there is no such thing as being too honest. So, what I am about to offer you is candid honest inside information! Use it well!

As a college professor, I certainly can testify to one simple fact about college professors: there is great variety among the herd. Any genius can tell you that there are "good people" and "bad people" in every group, from the professions through every other field. You most certainly have seen good teachers and bad teachers already, and in college, you will continue to find same. As a prospective college graduate, you must learn to differentiate among the various breeds, and deal with each accordingly. An informed discussion of several species of Talking Heads follows.

Without a doubt, you will meet "*The Intelligent Boobs.*" They usually have a very high opinion of themselves, higher than any objective assessment ever could justify! They often have little or no common sense, are difficult to talk to, rarely answer questions, and find students to be an annoyance. In the simplest terms, they are elitist, stuck up snobs. My feeling about members of this group is that they never should be allowed anywhere near people, let alone students. Unfortunately, some college administrators seem to love them, possibly because they bear a striking resemblance to themselves. You will have at least a few of these creatures as "teachers," so you may as well learn from the experience. Here are a few simple directives. Don't argue with them. Give them what they want. Do your work, go to class, pay attention, take notes, and avoid the idle chatter during class. (This is a good approach in any professor's class.) Remind yourself that you are not going to marry any of them; you simply need to complete the work for one of their courses. Finally, I found a simple mantra, mumbled under your breath, to be a great aid in dealing with these boors: "This person's an idiot; I just have to get my degree. This person's an idiot; I just have to get my degree." I can tell you, from years (and degrees) of experience: this mantra really works! This is not rocket science. Get through the course, do the best that you can, and continue on your life's journey.

Another type of college professor is *"The Upper Class and the Clueless."* These creatures have many of the same personality traits and character flaws as the intelligent boobs, but with an additional complicating factor: they are of a "privileged" social class background. They therefore are much less likely than yourself to know anyone well who actually "works for a living," like your parents and mine. They will not understand, nor care about, your financial situation and the time constraints that are **caused** by your financial situation. In fact, they have lived their lives sheltered from financial difficulties. Working class students like you and I must out of necessity work far more hours per week, at jobs, than professors or students from upper class backgrounds. The upper class and the clueless probably did not have to struggle as you are struggling to pay for college and everything else. In fact, they likely had their tuition and everything else handed to them on a silver platter. In your interactions and competition with the sons and daughters of the upper class and the clueless, however, you do have one distinct advantage. You are much more likely to have a strong work ethic than they are!

A third major type of professor is *"The Cliquer."* From my extensive experiences in higher education, I conclude that there are quite a few of this particular type out there. Like every other type of professor, cliquers absolutely come in both the female and male varieties. Style of dress and size of day planner sometimes are clues to their true identity. They definitely do not look like they ever waited tables or pushed a hand truck. This type of professor will appear to love students, since a select few students tend to congregate near their desks before and after their classes. The reality is, however, that these professors probably will not like you. Students of like ilk (*quiffy,* preppy, upper middle class high brow types) will follow them around like lost sheep with their border collie. These students will brown up to the professor, hoping to curry favors, better grades, and any other droppings they can find. You can tell immediately whether or not your professor is one of the cliquers or simply a "great teacher." Walk up to his desk after class, after the small crowd already has formed, and try to ask a question. If you get "quiffitude" (an interesting combination of anger and snobbery), or any other unpleasant reaction, drop the course immediately!

An additional type of professor is "*The Eager Beaver.*" These professors either are trying to make points with their administrators (for promotion or tenure), or simply are obsessed with their own (real or imagined) "expertise." They sometimes mean well, but almost always will overwork their students to death. Eager beavers give so much work that no one in her right mind ever could complete it all during a semester. They sometimes act as if their course is the only thing that students have to think about or work on. Usually, they simply cannot understand that you are not as excited about their courses as they are. They are difficult to reason with, and hard to please, but, if you are stuck with one, do your best to give him what he wants within reason. Fortunately, this breed is not too common. From my experience, quite a few eager beavers temper their enthusiasm, and adjust their courses' work loads, with some experience. A few others burn out, and many have the potential to evolve into good or great teachers.

A fifth major type of professor I have seen I call: "*The Good People, OK or Good Teachers.*" There are quite a few of this type. Because they are good people, they can be improved as teachers. As a student, it is your job to help them improve! If they are unclear, ask questions. (Always ask questions respectfully.) If they are going too fast, try to slow them down. If they do not write much on the board, encourage them to do so. Do a "learning styles inventory" for yourself, if you haven't already done so. Ask about this in student services or the counseling center. Then, adapt and adjust your learning approach to the various teaching styles that you encounter, and try to adapt, that is, improve your professors' teaching styles. If you are more of a visual learner (you learn best by seeing), take a lot of notes, and get every handout you can get. If you write slowly, or you are more of an auditory learner (you learn best by hearing), tape record classes (with permission). Push yourself to be the very best student that you can be, and do the same for your professors. Most good people are open to respectful suggestions, and many want to improve their teaching. Help them to teach better, and they in turn will help you learn.

"*The Great Teachers*" round out this discussion. They almost always are "good people." In fact, the most essential characteristic of great teachers is that they are "down to earth." They are relatively easy to find, since they stand out in the crowd of talking heads. They often are found surrounded by students, typically have numerous student office hours, and always are willing to offer help and advice, gently. They often are eminently qualified, but without the great egos. Although they have vastly differing teaching styles, they all share a genuine passion for their life's work. In fact, most of them do not even consider teaching to be "work." It is their calling, and they do it effortlessly, although many exhaust themselves in the process. They love interaction with students, but they should remain very conscious of clear boundaries, and maintaining them. Those who cross or blur boundaries should be avoided. When you find one of these people, latch on to her or him! (figuratively, please!) You can learn a great deal from great teachers, about rocket science, literature, and/or life. They willingly serve as mentors and role models for many students, and typically see that particular function as "the prime directive." They will help you adjust to college, graduate, and apply to graduate school. They will write you strong letters of recommendation, and help you to achieve your goals. If all professors were like these people, the college dropout rates would fall to near zero. Fortunately, there really are many "good" or "great" teachers in colleges and universities throughout American society.

The importance of good and great teachers to your success in college should not be underestimated. Most of the college student respondents in my "Life Stories" research, and many of my own college students, emphasized "having good teachers" when discussing these issues with me. As you take college courses, you should gravitate towards the good and great teachers, and minimize your exposure to the other types out there. You also should be seeking out mentors, professors who can help guide you, and teach you how to guide yourself, through the college success process. Look for people who remind you of the best teachers you have had before college, and of your most important teachers: your own parents. Open communication (again, with boundaries) is an extremely important component of a teacher/ student mentoring relationship. Remember: every one of your professors was a freshman once, and the best among your professors will draw from their own experiences to help you and to keep themselves "real" and humble. Successful college students usually have many more positive experiences with their teachers than negative ones. Do not ignore your role and your obligations in the process of becoming a college graduate. Never forget that a big part of that is: go to class and do your work, to the best of your ability and with substantial effort. Remember, it is easier not to go to college, but then, your life likely would be harder and much less fulfilling if you chose to skip college.

CHOOSING A MAJOR

"What do want to be when you grow up?" Once you reach college, that innocent childhood question asked of you by your sweet Aunt Emily becomes the prodding harassment of "When are you *finally* going to decide what you want to do?" Well meaning friends and relatives, know it all high school dropouts, and nosy neighbors alike constantly bombard you with that question, beginning five seconds after you get home from freshman orientation. In fact, this is probably why many freshmen declare their majors too quickly and hastily. Some of these people actually mean well, and some of them really want to help. Most of them simply cannot see that, when you are asked the same question six million times in three weeks, it gets old real fast. One of the most important things about going to college is to **graduate,** and so, that should be one of your primary goals. So, what do you tell all the well meaning pests, if you do not yet know what it is that you want to do? Tell them that you want to be a college graduate, leave it at that, and walk away. Run away, instead! Ultimately, choosing your field or major is your decision. So, when people offer their suggestions, take those suggestions with a grain of salt. Just because one of your uncles is a typewriter repairman does not mean that you want to become one.

Choosing a major, to most college students, looks like this earth-shattering, monumental, and irreversible decision that will affect the rest of their lives. Actually, it is not; it just looks that way. Choosing a major is a *process,* not a single decision. For most graduates, it happens over time, not in an instant. Events, courses, and other decisions and choices that you make eventually lead you to choose a major, but it is not one choice. It is a series of choices, twists and turns and forks in the road, that inevitably lead you to some major or field of study. It is very reversible, since many college graduates change their majors two or three times along the way. At many colleges, the form that you use to declare your major is the same form that you use to change your major. In addition, many graduates get jobs outside their respective fields of major anyway. If you think that you know what you want to do, take your shoes off, and jump in the water. The sooner you check out your possible major, the better. If you are not sure (and freshmen probably should not be sure), then sample. There are numerous fields and possible majors out there, so dabble and explore as a freshman. Your college likely requires every student to take a little of this, and a little of that, as their general education requirements for all majors and degrees. So, treat your freshman year as if you were going to a huge, all you can eat buffet. Savor. Sample. Explore. Check various dishes out. Start with what you think you like, and stay away from what you do not like. If you take, say, an introductory psychology course in your first semester, and you really like it, then take another psychology course in your next semester. If, after a couple of psychology courses, you still want more, then, maybe it's psychology. Be realistic. Know yourself. Find out what the choices are, and look into as many as you can. Then, the major chooses you! Do not worry. It will work out. Most college graduates worried about choosing their majors, but they went on to graduate anyway. In time, you will join them. Give yourself that time, and enjoy the search. It is a great part of the college experience, the exploring.

In the twenty first century, most young adult college graduates eventually will work for several different employers and in several different fields during their working lifetimes. Changing fields is the norm today, as is getting jobs outside your field of major. You do not need to know what you want to do for the rest of your life when you are choosing a major. You only want to know what your major is going to be, unless you later change it! Most majors lead to jobs in many different fields, and majoring in something that you find interesting will dramatically improve your chances of graduating and earning that degree. Obviously, if you want to be a nurse, you should not major in sociology. (I have had quite a few nursing majors minor in sociology.) Many college graduates find out what they really want to do after they graduate by actually doing it after they graduate. Internships, part time jobs, and service learning activities sometimes give students cues and clues. Finding and doing a few different full time jobs after graduation often helps graduates find their careers. Do not get too far ahead of yourself; concentrate on doing your schoolwork and graduating, until you are reasonably certain that you will be graduating. Once you have your degree, you then will be eligible to apply for jobs that are significantly higher up the food chain than most high school graduates' job prospects typically are.

GRADUATE SCHOOL, ANYONE?

Once you have earned your four year degree, you then will enjoy the possibility of applying for graduate and professional programs. There are several simple rules of thumb that then are apropos. The last degree that you earn typically is the most important, so your goal should be to move up. For many students, it is fine (and a good choice) to begin their college studies at a local two year community college. You then use the Associate's (two year) degree as a stepping stone to the Bachelor's degree. If you earn your Bachelor's degree from a second tier school, you should work to enter the graduate program of a first tier institution. If you earn your four year degree from one of the "better" colleges or universities, then think about applying to some top ten or top twenty schools for your Master's. Your cum will influence what your various options are, but never assume that you can't get into the school of your dreams. Apply, and let them tell you if you are "unworthy." If (surprise!) you get in, go!!! If they accepted you, then they assume that you can do it. You accept their invitation, you go, (buy some "better" clothes, if you must) and then, you simply do what students do (and what you have done successfully to this point).

I was shocked and in awe when I first attended Columbia University. I adjusted, and I had an amazing experience. It really is an *amazing* place. When I mention applying to elite universities like Columbia to my students, their shocked looks are all too familiar to me. They apply, and more than a few are shocked again when they receive acceptance letters.

At this point, immediately after reading this brief section of this book, I know what you are thinking: "I am still in high school." I mention graduate school in my introductory sociology class that typically has many freshmen in it when we discuss social mobility (movement up or down in social class). Most of my students look at me like I finally lost my mind. In three years, more than a few of them are seeking me out to request letters of recommendation for a Master's program! So there! Text that to your friends and relatives!

When you do go to grad school, you may choose to earn a Master's or professional degree in a different field than your Bachelor's degree. For example, many students for whom I had written letters of recommendation earned Master's degrees in social work after completing Bachelor's degrees in psychology, sociology, or social sciences. They are not eligible for advanced standing programs, and so, they typically complete four semesters of field placements in graduate school. Many college graduates who decide to become teachers earn Master's degrees in education without having been education majors as undergraduates. There are countless other examples. The key point is that the Bachelor's degree rarely is a terminal degree; you always can go on to a Master's degree in something. The beauty of becoming a four year college graduate is that you increase the number of positive, win/win choices that you then will have for the rest of your life, and that is a good thing.

REMIND YOURSELF WHY EVERY DAY

By deciding to attend college, you already have decided that there are many things that you do not want to do with your life. *Remind* yourself about some of those things, and **why** you do not want to do them. For many college students, that is easy, because they work part or full time at various dead end jobs as they earn their degrees. You need to remind yourself of your long term goal (to earn your four year degree, at least), to help you get through some of the days and courses that will drag. You are putting in all this hard work now so that the rest of your life will be easier and more rewarding, emotionally and financially. The easiest time to do this college thing is when you are a young adult, and still living at home. It only gets harder if you have to support yourself and/or a family, too. Ask any returning adult college student about that! Many of them get their degrees despite working full time, going to school, and caring for their families. If you are living at home (or in a dorm), and working part time, you have it easy, relatively speaking. Ultimately, you are putting in all these hours of work and study for yourself, so do it for yourself. If you earn your four year degree, you then could go on to any advanced, graduate, or professional degree, and the world would be your oyster. Without a four year degree, a young adult American in the twenty first century likely should expect life to be a **lifetime** struggle. Ultimately, the choice is **yours**.

APPENDIX

Introduction

The interviews were conducted in 1990, 1991, and 1992. Generally, although I followed the format of the interview schedule (the list of questions) while conducting each interview, I always encouraged each respondent to talk about whatever the respondent wanted to talk about, in response to any specific question. I conducted each interview in a similar manner, asking the same questions in the same order. Many of the questions were somewhat closed ended. This means that respondents had to choose from a short list of possible answers (like age or birth order). Other questions were much more open ended. This means that respondents could answer by saying anything that came to mind. This gave them the opportunity to describe realities in great detail, and give me explanations and feelings in their answers. During each interview, I used probes and follow up questions liberally (to get more information and more detailed information), and whenever a respondent was unclear or evasive. Occasionally, one question in the interview schedule was similar to another. This served as a double check. Data concerning open communication between the student respondents and their parents, and the degree of upward mobility among the respondents' parents came from respondents' answers to several questions each, as well as from their general comments. Generalizations frequently were based on several responses or comments by each respondent. The interview schedule itself follows.

Interview Schedule

Family Experiences:

1. Growing up, how often did you see your cousins, aunts, and uncles?
2. What was it like financially growing up?
3. Growing up, how did your parents react if you did something wrong?
4. How did your parents feel about education?
5. Did anyone help you with your schoolwork?
6. Did you have books or encyclopedias at home?
7. Did anyone help you with college expenses or tuition?
8. Did you take out loans, or get scholarships or other financial aid?
9. Describe your relationships with your parents.
10. Who was in charge at home?
11. Who usually did what?
12. What were your responsibilities at home?
13. How important were material things?
14. What did you like about living at home?
15. What did you dislike about living at home?
16. What were your parents interests or hobbies?
17. What were your interests or hobbies?
18. How well organized were your parents?
19. Were your parents very religious?
20. What problems or tensions were there at home?

Parents' Work Experiences:

1. What were your father's jobs? (including work history)
2. Describe what your father does (or did) on his job.
3. How does he feel about the job?
4. How deeply into his work is your father?
5. Does he do odd jobs, or tinker?

6. Does he work for a small company, large company, or for himself, and for how long?
7. How often has he been laid off or hurt on the job?
8. Would you say that your father's main loyalty is to his employer, or to his craft or trade?

NOTE: Questions 1 – 8 were repeated concerning the respondent's mother. If the respondent's mother was not employed outside the home, I asked the respondent to discuss in detail what her or his mother usually did.

Respondent's Work Experiences:

1. Do you work? If yes, approximately how many hours per week?
2. Describe what kind of job you have, and what you do at work. (including work history)
3. Tell me about your work experiences.
4. Tell me about your experiences with bosses and coworkers.
5. Were you ever laid off or hurt on the job?

Friends and Others:

1. Do your brothers and sisters go to college?
2. How many of your friends go to college?
3. Did your best friend from high school go to college?
4. Did your serious girlfriend or boyfriend from high school go to college?
5. Did anyone else you are close to go to college, or stress education? (in addition to parents)
6. How many of your cousins went to college?
7. Describe the crowds you "hung out with" growing up.

School Experiences:

1. Did you go to public, private, or parochial schools?
2. Tell me about your school experiences through high school.
3. How did teachers treat you?
4. How did other students treat you?

Asked of All College Attenders:

1. Tell me about your college experiences.
2. Did you live on your own or with your parents while you attended college?
3. How do (or did) you feel about college?
4. What is (or was) your schedule like?
5. Did you have enough time to do everything that you had to do, or that you wanted to do?
6. How do (or did) you cope, when you don't (or didn't) have enough time?
7. Why did you go to college?
8. If respondent left college: Why did you leave college?

Asked of All Nonattenders:

1. Did you think about going to college?
2. Why didn't you go to college?

Background:

1. Do you live on your own or with your parents?
2. Presently, are you married, divorced, or single?
3. Do you have any children? Ages?
4. When you were growing up, did your parents own their own home, rent, or live with other relatives?

5. Have either of your parents passed away? If yes, did they re-main married until one died?
6. Are your parents still married?
7. How many sisters and brothers do you have?
8. Are you the oldest, middle, or youngest?
9. How old are you?
10. How old are your siblings?

Student Respondents Only:

1. What year are you in college?
2. Did you transfer from another school?
3. Do you have a major?
4. At this point, what is your career or possible career?

All Respondents:

1. What is your racial or ethnic background?
2. How important is your racial or ethnic background to you?
3. What is your religious background?
4. How important is your religious background to you?

REFERENCES

Alexander, C.N., Jr., and E.Q. Campbell. (1964). Peer Influences on Adolescent Educational Aspirations. *American Sociological Review*, Vol. 29:568-575.

Alexander, Karl L., Martha Cook, and Edward L. McDill. (1978). Curriculum Tracking and Educational Stratification: Some Further Evidence. *American Sociological Review*, Vol. 43 (February):47-66.

Alexander, Karl L., Aaron M. Pallas, and Scott Holupka. (1987). *Consistency and Change in Educational Stratification. Research in Social Stratification and Mobility*, Vol. 6:161-185.

Alwin, D. and A. Thornton. (1984). Family Origins and the Schooling Process. *American Sociological Review*, Vol. 49:784-802.

Anderson, Elijah. (1999). Code of the Street. New York: W.W. Norton.

Anderson, R.C., et al. (1985). Becoming a Nation of Readers. Urbana, Illinois: University of Illinois Center for the Study of Reading.

Apple, Michael W. (1982). *Education and Power: Reproduction and Contradiction in Education*. London: Routledge and Kegan Paul.

Aronowitz, Stanley. (1973). False Promises: *The Shaping of American Working Class Consciousness*. New York: McGraw Hill.

Astin, Alexander W. (1975). *Preventing Students From Dropping Out*. San

Francisco: Jossey-Bass.

Astin, Alexander W. et al. (1988). *The American Freshman National Norms for Fall 1988.* Los Angeles: Higher Education Research Institute, University of California, Los Angeles.

Ballantine, Jeanne H. (1989). *Schools and Society.* Mountain View, California: Mayfield Publishing.

Becher, Rhoda McShane. (1984). *Parental Involvement: A Review of Research and Principles of Successful Practice.* Washington, D.C.: National Institute of Education.

Becker, H.J., and J. Epstein. (1982). Parent Involvement: A Survey of Teacher Practices. *The Elementary School Journal*, Vol. 83, No. 2:85-102.

Berger, Peter, and Thomas Luckmann. (1966). *The Social Construction of Reality.* Garden City, New York: Doubleday.

Blau, Peter M., and Otis Dudley Duncan. (1967). *The American Occupational Structure.* New York: Free Press.

Blauner, Robert. (1964). *Alienation and Freedom.* Chicago: University of Chicago Press.

Blondal, Kristjana S., and Sigrun Adalbjarnardottir. (2009). Parenting Practices and School Dropout: A Longitudinal Study. *Adolescence*, Vol. 44, Iss. 176 (Winter):729-749.

Bloom, B.S., editor. (1985). *Developing Talent in Young People.* New York: Ballantine Books.

Bloom, B.S., and L.A. Sosniak. (1981). Talent Development vs. Schooling. *Educational Leadership*, Vol. 39, No. 2:86-94.

Bluestone, Barry, and Bennett Harrison. (1982). *The Deindustrialization of America.* New York: Basic Books.

Bottomore, T. B.. *Classes in Modern Soiciety.* (1966). New York: Random

House.

Bowles, Samuel, and Herbert Gintis. (1976). *Schooling in Capitalist America*. New York: Basic Books.

Bowles, Samuel, David M. Gordon, and Thomas Weisskopf. (1984). *Beyond the Waste Land*. Garden City, New York: Doubleday.

Boyer, Richard O., and Herbert M. Morais. (1973). *Labor's Untold Story*. New York: United Electrical, Radio, and Machine Workers of America.

Bronfenbrenner, Urie. (1974). *A Report on Longitudinal Evaluations Of Preschool Programs, Vol. II: Is Early Intervention Effective?* Washington, D.C.: Office of Child Development, Department of Health, Education, and Welfare.

Brophy, J.E. (1981). Teacher Praise: A Functional Analysis. *Review of Education Research*, Vol. 51:5-32.

Burawoy, Michael. *Manufacturing Consent*. (1979). Chicago: University of Chicago Press.

Bureau of the Census. (2010; 2000; 1990). *Statistical Abstract of the United States*. Washington, D.C.: U.S. Government Printing Office.

Carpenter, Peter G., and John A. Fleishman. (1987). Linking Intentions and Behavior: Australian Students' College Plans and College Attendance. *American Educational Research Journal*, Vol. 24, No. 1 (Spring):79-105.

Chomsky, C. (1972). *Stages in Language Development and Reading Exposure*. Harvard Educational Review, Vol. 42:1-33.

Clark, Reginald M. (1983). *Family Life and School Achievement*. Chicago: University of Chicago Press.

Cohen, Jere. (1987). Parents as Educational Models and Definers. *Journal of Marriage and the Family*, Vol. 49 (May):339-351.

Colclough, Glenna, and E.M. Beck. (1986). The American Educational Structure and the Reproduction of Social Class. *Sociological Inquiry*, Vol. 56 (Fall):456-76.

Coleman, James S., et al. (1966). *Equality of Educational Opportunity.* Washington, D.C.: U.S. Government Printing Office.

Coleman, James S., and Thomas Hoffer. (1987). *Public and Private High Schools: The Impact of Communities.* New York: Basic Books.

Coleman, James S., Thomas Hoffer, and Sally Kilgore. (1982). *High School Achievement: Public, Catholic, and Private Schools Compared.* New York: Basic Books.

Coleman, Richard P., and Lee Rainwater, with Kent A. McClelland. (1978). *Social Standing in America: New Dimensions of Class.* New York: Basic Books.

Collins, Randall. (1979). *The Credential Society.* New York: Academic Press.

Conant, James B. *Slums and Suburbs.* (1961). New York: McGraw Hill.

Conklin, Mary E., and Ann Ricks Dailey. (1981). Does Consistency of Educational Encouragement Matter for Secondary School Students? *Sociology of Education*, Vol. 54 (October):254-262.

Dahrendorf, Ralf. (1959). *Class and Class Conflict in Industrial Society.* Stanford, California: Stanford University Press.

Dahrendorf, Ralf. (1979). *Life Chances.* Chicago: University of Chicago Press.

Davis, James A., and Tom W. Smith. (1988). *General Social Surveys, 1972-1988: Cumulative Codebook.* Chicago: National Opinion Research Center.

Demo, David H., and Ritch C. Savin-Williams. (1983). Early Adolescent Self Esteem as a Function of Social Class: Rosenberg and Pearlin Revisited. *American Journal of Sociology*, Vol. 88, No. 4 (January):763-

774.

Dey, Eric L. et al. (1991). *The American Freshman: Twenty-Five Year Trends*. Los Angeles: Higher Education Research Institute, University of California, Los Angeles.

Doeringer, Peter, and Michael Piore. (1971). *Internal Labor Markets and Manpower Analysis*. Lexington, Massachusetts: D. C. Heath.

Domhoff, G. William. (1983). *Who Rules America Now?* Englewood Cliffs, New Jersey: Prentice-Hall.

Dornbusch, Sanford, et al. (1987). *The Relation of Parenting Style to Adolescent School Performance*. Child Development, Vol. 58 (October):1244-1257.

Dornbusch, Sanford. (1986). *Helping Your Kid Make the Grade.Palo Alto*, California: The Stanford Magazine.

Duberman, Lucille. (1976). *Social Inequality: Caste and Class in America*. Philadelphia: Lippincott.

Duncan, Otis Dudley, David L. Featherman, and Beverly Duncan. (1972). *Socioeconomic Background and Achievement*. New York: Academic Press.

Dunn, N.E. (1981). Children's Achievement at School-Entry Age as a Function of Mothers' and Fathers' Teaching Sets. *The Elementary School Journal*, Vol. 81:245-253.

Edsall, Thomas B. (1988). *The Return of Inequality*. Atlantic Monthly, (June): 89.

Fischer, Claude S. et al. (1977). *Networks and Places*. New York: Free Press.

Forer, L. and Henry Still. (`1976). *The Birth Order Factor*s. New York: David McKay.

Fussell, Paul. *Class*. (1983). New York: Ballantine Books.

Gaines, Donna. (1991). *Teenage Wasteland: Suburbia's Dead End Kids.* New York: Pantheon.

Gans, Herbert J. (1982). *The Levittowners.* New York: Columbia University Press.

Gans, Herbert. (1973). *More Equality.* New York: Random House.

Giddens, Anthony. (1973). *The Class Structure of the Advanced Societies.* New York: Harper and Row.

Giddens, Anthony, and David Held, editors. (1982). *Class, Power, and Conflict.* Berkeley: University of California Press.

Ginsburg, A., and S. Hanson. (1985). *Gaining Ground: Values and High School Success.* Washington, D.C.: U.S. Department of Education.

Good, T.L. (1982). *How Teachers' Expectations Affect Results.American Education*, Vol. 18 (December):25-32.

Good, T.L., and Brophy, J.E. (1984). *Looking in Classrooms.* New York: Harper and Row.

Graue, M.E., T. Weinstein, and H.J. Walberg. (1983). School-based Home Instruction and Learning: A Quantitative Synthesis. *Journal of Educational Research*, Vol. 76:351-360.

Granfield, Robert. (1991). *Making It By Faking It. Journal of Contemporary Ethnography*, Vol. 20, No. 3 (October):331-351.

Granfield, Robert, and T. Koenig. (1990). From Activism to Pro Bono: Redirecting of Working Class Altruism at Harvard Law School. *Critical Sociology*, Vol. 17:57-80.

Grusky, David B., and Robert M. Hauser. (1984). Comparative Social Mobility Revisited: Models of Convergence and Divergence in 16 Countries. *American Sociological Review*, 49):19-38.

Halle, David. (1984). *America's Working Man.* Chicago: University of Chicago Press.

Hauser, Robert M., and David L. Featherman. (1977). *The Process of Stratification*. New York: Academic Press.

Hauser, Robert M., and David B. Grusky. (1988). Cross-National Variation in Occupational Distributions, Relative Mobility Chances, and Intergenerational Shifts in Occupational Distributions. *American Sociological Review*, 53:723-741.

Heath, S.B. (1983). *Ways with Words: Language, Life, and Work in Communities and Classrooms*. New York: Cambridge University Press.

Heller, Celia. (1969). *Structured Social Inequality*. New York: Macmillan.

Henderson, Anne, ed. (1987). *The Evidence Continues to Grow: Parental Involvement Improves Student Achievement.* Columbia, Maryland: National Committee for Citizens in Education.

Henry, Carolyn S., Michael J. Merten, Scott W. Plunkett, and Tovah Sands. (2008). Neighborhood, Parenting, and Adolescent Factors and Academic Achievement in Latino Adolescents From Immigrant Families. *Family Relations*, Vol. 57 , Iss 5(Dec.):579-590.

Herbers, Janette E., J. J. Cutuli, Theresa L. Lafavor, Danielle Vrieze, Cari Leibel, Jelena Obradovic, and Ann S. Masten. Direct and Indirect Effects of Parenting on the Academic Functioning of Young Homeless Children. (2011). *Early Education and Development*, Vol. 22, Iss. 1:77.

Hochschild, Arlie, and Anne Machung. (1989). *The Second Shift: Working Parents and the Revolution at Home*. New York: Penguin Books.

Hodge, Robert W., Paul M. Siegal, and Peter H. Rossi. (1966). Occupational Prestige in the United States: 1925-1963. In Reinhard Bendix and Seymour Martin Lipset (Editors), *Class, Status, and Power.* New York: Free Press.

Homans, George. (1974). *Social Behavior: Its Elementary Forms.* Revised Edition. New York: Harcourt Brace Jovanovich.

Hood, Jane. (1983). *Becoming a Two Job Family*. New York: Praeger.

Hotchkiss, Lawrence, and Linda Eberst Dorsten. (1987). Curriculum Effects on Early Post-High School Outcomes. *Research in Sociology of Education and Socialization*, Vol. 7:191-219.

Howe, Louise Kapp. (1977). *Pink Collar Workers*. New York: Putnam.

Howell, Joseph T. (1973). *Hard Living on Clay Street*. Garden City, New York: Doubleday.

Hurn, Christopher. (1985). *The Limits and Possibilities of Schooling*. 2nd edition. Boston: Allyn and Bacon.

Jencks, Christopher, and David Riesman. (1968). *The Academic Revolution*. Garden City, New York: Doubleday.

Jencks, Christopher et al. (1972). *Inequality*. New York: Basic Books.

Jencks, Christopher. (1979). *Who Gets Ahead?* New York: Basic Books.

Kanter, Rosabeth Moss. (1977). *Men and Women of the Corporation*. New York: Basic Books.

Karabel, Jerome. (1972). Community Colleges and Social Stratification. *Harvard Educational Review*, Vol. 42, No. 4 (November):521-562.

Karp, David A.. (1986). You Can Take the Boy Out of Dorchester, but You Can't Take the Dorchester Out of the Boy. *Symbolic-Interaction*, Vol. 9, No. 1 (Spring):19-36.

Keith, T.Z. (1982). Time Spent on Homework and High School Grades: A Large-Sample Path Analysis. *Journal of Educational Psychology*, Vol. 74, No. 2 (April):248-253.

Keniston, Kenneth. (1977). *All Our Children*. New York: Carnegie Corporation.

Kerbo, Harold R. (2009). *Social Stratification and Inequality*. (Seventh Edition) New York: McGraw Hill.

Kirk, Chris Michael, Rhonda K. Lewis-Moss, Corinne Nilsen, and Deltha Colvin. (2011). The Role of Parental Expectations on Adolescent Educational Aspirations. *Educational Studies*, Vol. 37, Iss. 1(Feb.):89.

Kiyosaki, Robert, with Sharon Lechter. (1997). *Rich Dad Poor Dad.* New York: Warner Books.

Kluegel, James R., and Eliot R. Smith. (1986). *Beliefs About Inequality.* New York: Aldine de Gruyter.

Kohn, Melvin L. (1977). *Class and Conformity.* Chicago: University of Chicago Press.

Komarovsky, Mirra. (1962). *Blue Collar Marriage.* New York: Random House.

Komarovsky, Mirra. (1985). *Women in College.* New York: Basic Books.

Kozol, Jonathan. (1968). *Death at an Early Age.* New York: Bantam.

Kozol, Jonathan. (1991). *Savage Inequalities.* New York: HarperCollins.

Kraus, Henry. (1985). *The Many and the Few.* Urbana, Illinois: University of Illinois Press.

Ladd, Everett, and Seymour Martin Lipset. (1977). *Survey of the American Professorate: Selected Tabulations.* Storrs: Social Science Data Center.

Lewis, Michael. (1978). *The Culture of Inequality.* New York: New American Library.

Lipset, Seymour Martin. (1972). *Social Mobility and Equal Opportunity.* Public Interest, 29 (Fall):90-108.

Lipset, Seymour Martin, editor. (1979). *The Third Century: America as a Postindustrial Society.* Chicago: University of Chicago Press.

Lipset, Seymour Martin, and Reinhard Bendix. (1959). *Social Mobility in Industrial Society.* Berkeley: University of California Press.

Lopez-Turley, Ruth N., Matthew Desmond, and Sarah K. Bruch. (2010).

Unanticipated Educational Consequences of a Positive Parent-Child Relationship. *Journal of Marriage and Family*, Vol. 72, Iss. 5(Oct.):1377-1390.

Maurer, Harry. (1979). Not Working: *An Oral History of the Unemployed.* New York: Holt, Rinehart, and Winston.

Mayeske, George W. (1973). *A Study of the Achievement of Our Nation's Students.* Washington, D.C.: U.S. Department of Health, Education, and Welfare.

Melville, Keith. (1988). *Marriage and Family Today.* New York: Random House.

Merton, Robert K. (1968). *Social Theory and Social Structure.* Second edition. New York: Free Press.

Mills, Charles Wright. (1956). *The Power Elite.* New York: Oxford University Press.

Mills, Charles Wright. (1959). *The Sociological Imagination.* New York: Oxford University Press.

Mindel, Charles H., Robert W. Habenstein, and Roosevelt Wright, Jr. (1998). *Ethnic Families in America.* Fourth edition. Upper Saddle River, New Jersey: Prentice-Hall.

Molloy, John T. (1975). *Dress for Success.* New York: Peter H. Wyden.

Molloy, John T. (1977). *The Women's Dress for Success Book.* New York: Warner Books.

Murray, Christopher. (2009). Parent and Teacher Relationships as Predictors of School Engagement and Functioning Among Low-Income Urban Youth. *The Journal of Early Adolescence*, Vol. 29, Iss. 3(Jun.):376-404.

National Center for Education Statistics. *Digest of Education Statistics.* (1992). Washington, D.C.: U.S. Department of Education.

Nebbitt, Von E., Margaret Lombe, Velma LaPoint, and Dawn Bryant. Predictors and Correlates of Academic Performance Among Urban African American Adolescents. (2009). *The Journal of Negro Education,* Vol.78, Iss. 1 (Winter):29-41.

Neubeck, Kenneth J., and Mary Alice Neubeck (1997). *Social Problems A Critical Approach.* Fourth edition. New York: McGraw-Hill.

Newman, Katherine S. (1993). *Declining Fortunes.* New York: Basic Books.

Newman, Katherine S. (1988). *Falling from Grace.* New York: Random House.

Noll, James William. (1989). *Taking Sides.* Guilford, Connecticut: Dushkin.

Oakes, Jeannie. (1985). *Keeping Track.* New Haven: Yale University Press.

Orthner, Dennis K., Hinckley Jones-Sanpei, Elizabeth C. Hair, and Kristin A. Moore, Randal D. Day, and Kelleen Kaye. (2009). Marital and Parental Relationship Quality and Educational Outcomes for Youth. *Marriage and Family Review*, Vol. 45, Iss. 2/3(Feb.):249-269.

Palley, Marian Lief. (1984). Reaganomics and Class Cleavages in the United States. *Journal of Politics*, Vol. 46 (August):938-46.

Parenti, Michael. (1978). *Power and the Powerless.* New York: St. Martins's Press.

Persell, Caroline Hodges. (1977). *Education and Inequality.* New York: Free Press.

Piven, Frances Fox, and Richard A. Cloward. (1982). *The New Class War.* New York: Pantheon.

Plunkett, Scott W., Andrew O. Behnke, Tovah Sands, and Brian Y. Choi. (2009). Adolescents' Reports of Parental Engagement and Academic Achievement in Immigrant Families. *Journal of Youth and Adolescence*, Vol. 38, Iss.2(Feb.):257-268.

Reich, Michael, David M. Gordon, and Richard C. Edwards. (1977). A Theory of Labor Market Segmentation. In David M. Gordon (Editor) *Problems in Political Economy*. Lexington, Massachusetts: D.C. Heath.

Rich, D.K. (1985). *The Forgotten Factor in School Success: the Family*. Washington, D.C.: Home and School Institute.

Rosenthal, Robert, and Lenore Jacobson. (1968). *Pygmalion in the Classroom*. New York: Holt, Rinehart, and Winston.

Rubin, Lillian Breslow. (1983). *Intimate Strangers*. New York: Harper and Row.

Rubin, Lillian Breslow. (1976). *Worlds of Pain*. New York: Basic Books.

Russo, Michael S. and Meritta Cullinan. (2006). *Surviving College*. Rockville Centre: Molloy College.

Rutchick, Abraham M., Joshua M. Smyth, Leonard M. Lopoo, and Jerome B. Dusek. (2009). Great Expectations: The Biasing Effects of Reported Child Behavior Problems on Educational Expectancies and Subsequent Academic Achievement. *Journal of Social and Clinical Psychology*, Vol. 28, Iss. 3(Mar.): 392-413.

Ryan, Jake, and Charles Sackrey. (1984). *Strangers in Paradise*. Boston: South End Press.

Ryan, William. (1976). *Blaming the Victim*. New York: Vintage.

Ryan, William. (1981). *Equality*. New York: Pantheon.

Ryan, William. Savage Discovery: The Moynihan Report. (1967) In Lee Rainwater and William L. Yancey (Editors) *The Moynihan Report and the Politics of Controversy*. Cambridge, Massachusetts: M.I.T. Press.

Santaniello, Michael A. (1995). *Beating the Odds: College Attenders and Nonattenders from the Working Class*. Ann Arbor, MI: UMI. (The "Life Stories" Research).

Schwarz, John E. and Thomas J. Volgy. (1992). *The Forgotten Americans: Thirty Million Working Poor in the Land of Opportunity*. (1992). New York: Norton.

Sennett, Richard, and Jonathan Cobb. (1973). *The Hidden Injuries of Class*. New York: Random House.

Sewell, William H., and Robert M. Hauser. (1975). *Education, Opportunity, and Earnings*. New York: Academic Press.

Sewell, William H., and Robert M. Hauser, editors. (1976). *Schooling and Achievement in American Society*. New York: Academic Press.

Sewell, William S., Robert M. Hauser, and Wendy C. Wolf. (1980). Sex, Schooling, and Occupational Status. *American Journal of Sociology*, 86:551-583.

Sewell, William H., and Vimal P. Shah. (1968). Social Class, Encouragement, and Educational Stratification. *American Journal of Sociology*, Vol. 73 (March):559-572.

Shor, Ira. (1987). Critical Teaching and Everyday Life. Chicago: University of Chicago Press.

Silberman, Charles E. (1971). *Crisis in the Classroom*. New York: Vintage.

Snarey, John R., and George E. Vaillant. (1985). *How Lower- and Working-Class Youth Become Middle-Class Adults*. Child Development, Vol. 56:899-910.

Spera, Christopher, Kathryn R. Wentzel, and Holly C. Matto. (2009). Parental Aspirations for Their Children's Educational Attainment: Relations to Ethnicity, Parental Education, Children's Academic Performance, and Parental Perceptions of School Climate. *Journal of Youth and Adolescence*, Vol. 38, Iss. 8(Sep.):1140-1152.

Stage, Frances K., and Don Hossler. (1989). Differences in Family Influences on College Attendance Plans for Male and Female Ninth Graders. *Research in Higher Education,* Vol. 30, No. 3 (June):301-315.

S.U.N.Y. at Stony Brook. *Undergraduate Bulletin.* (1991).

Straus, Murray A., Richard J. Gelles, and Suzanne K. Steinmetz. (1980). *Behind Closed Doors*. Garden City, New York: Doubleday.

Steinitz, V., and E. Solomon. (1986). *Starting Out: Class and Community in the Lives of Working Class Youth.* Philadelphia: Temple University Press. Suffolk County Community College. Catalog. (1993-1994).

Trussel, J. (1988). *Teenage Pregnancy in the United States.* Family Planning Perspectives, 20:262-272.

Turner, Erlanger A., Megan Chandler, and Robert W. Heffer. (2009). The Influence of Parenting Styles, Achievement Motivation, and Self-Efficacy on Academic Performance in College Students. *Journal of College Student Development,* Vol. 50, Iss.3(May/June):337-346.

U.S. Bureau of Labor Statistics, U.S. Department of Labor. *Occupational Outlook Handbook,* 2010-11 Library Edition. Washington, D.C., Superintendent of Documents, U.S. Government Printing Office.

U.S. Bureau of Labor Statistics, *U.S. Department of Labor. Occupational Outlook Handbook,* 2004-05 Library Edition. Washington, D.C., Superintendent of Documents, U.S. Government Printing Office.

Valentine, Charles A. (1968). *Culture and Poverty.* Chicago, University of Chicago Press.

Walberg, H.J. (1985). *Homework's Powerful Effects on Learning. Educational Leadership*, Vol. 42, No. 7:76-79.

Walberg, H.J. (1984). Improving the Productivity of America's Schools. *Educational Leadership*, Vol. 41, No. 8:19-27.

Willis, Paul. (1977). *Learning to Labor: How Working Class Kids Get Working Class Jobs.* New York: Columbia University Press.

Young, Michael. (1961). *The Rise of the Meritocracy.* New York: Penguin Books.

Mike Santaniello, Ph.D. is an Associate Professor of Sociology at Molloy College. Dr. Mike earned a Bachelor's degree in sociology at Stony Brook University, and two Master's degrees and a Ph.D. in sociology at Columbia University. Dr. Mike published his doctoral dissertation, *Beating the Odds: College Attenders and Nonattenders from the Working Class*, in 1995.

24290880R00107

Made in the USA
Columbia, SC
25 August 2018